BASKETBALL
THE DREAM GAME IN KENTUCKY

DAVE KINDRED

The Courier-Journal
The Louisville Times

Data Courier, Inc.

Executive Editor:
Robert E. Deitz

Editor:
William S. Butt

Book Design:
Dan Stewart, Harriet Winner
Designers Stewart and Winner
Louisville, Kentucky

Published by Data Courier, Inc.,
for *The Courier-Journal* and
The Louisville Times

Production Manager:
Carmen Chetti

Library of Congress Catalog
Number: 75-31042

Printer:
Fetter Printing Company
Louisville, Kentucky
First Printing December, 1975

CONTENTS

INTRODUCTION

Being born and reared in Illinois is almost as unfortunate as, well, being a blasted *Hoosier*, for heaven's sake. But Dave Kindred has overcome this horrible accident of birth remarkably well. Ever since he first came to work for The Courier-Journal in 1965, Dave has plunged into the wonderful world of Kentucky basketball with a passion and spirit that even the most loyal native would be hard-pressed to match. Even more importantly, he has written about it with the wit, style, grace, and economy of words that, in my humble opinion, has made him one of the finest journalists, sports or otherwise, punching typewriter keys on the American newspaper scene today.

Too often, there is a shocking gap between sports writers and other kinds of journalists. True, some of America's finest writers — James Reston and Jimmy Breslin come to mind right away — began their careers in sports writing. However, for the most part, sports writers too often seem a bit lazier, a bit less inquisitive, a bit less willing to pursue the truth, than their colleagues on the city or state desks. Not so Kindred. Ever since I have known

him, which is a decade or so now, Dave has looked at sports not only with the loving eye of a fan, but also with the keen, critical perspective of a professional reporter. Sometimes, this hasn't made him the most popular man in the state. Once, at a party, a guy stood in front of me and began to lambast Dave for one transgression or another. Emboldened by a few sips of Kentucky's finest, I tilted toward him and said, "Listen, buddy, you're lucky to have a guy like Kindred around here and don't forget it." I meant that, and I still do.

For a fan of Kindred, or, mostly, just a fan of basketball in Kentucky, the book that you are about to read is a jewel. I'm not just saying that because I'm a friend of Dave's, or because I was paid hand-somely to write this introduction (hah!). I'm saying it because I have read the book, and was amazed at how much I didn't know about this sport that has been so much a part of my life for 25 years or so, ever since I was a kid in Lexington who thought that the world's holiest place was not the Vatican, but UK's Memorial Coliseum.

Until I read Dave's book, I thought I

knew about as much as there was to know about Adolph Rupp, King Kelly Coleman, Ralph Beard, the Kentucky Colonels. Wrong. Thanks to those Kindred trademarks — diligence and sensitivity to detail — the legends have come alive in a fresh, exciting way. I defy any true basketball lover to read the poignant story of Ralph Beard without getting a basketball in the throat. I defy the same lover to read the chapters about Rupp and the fans without pausing every few lines to howl with laughter. Even the stuff I already knew, or had read, was fun to read again, such is Dave's mastery of the language. Sometimes, as when he writes of a country boy bouncing his basketball home, past "Cattle on hilltops (that) stood on the day's last, thin, redding sunbeams," Kindred's prose becomes poetry.

At this point, I've got to interject a couple of negative things about the author, lest you think I'm writing a puff piece here. For one thing, Kindred is awful to play basketball with. He's got this jump shot — actually, it's more of a hop-and-skip shot — that he shoots with depressing regularity. In a game, I've tried to discourage him through the use of various insults, scowls and intimidating gestures. It's no good. As soon as the ball hits his hands, it's gone. If Pete Maravich was a pistol, Kindred is at least a Gatling gun.

I also am not sure I agree with his all-time Kentucky college team that you may find in the final chapter. When it comes to strictly clutch players, how can you leave off Vernon Hatton of UK? Doesn't Kindred remember 1958, when Hatton twice beat Guy Rodgers and Temple with impossible last-second shots?

Finally, he did all that writing about his mediocrity as a high school player, but he failed to mention my (brief) career with the Park Methodist Bluejays of Lexington. I wore No. 23, which, as I recall, was what Frank Ramsey was wearing for the Boston Celtics in those days. Our colors were blue and white, just like UK. We even had a cheerleader, the minister's daughter, whose timid "Come on, Blue Jays, We want a basket" whispers in my mind to this day.

In one memorable game, I was the only substitute. For three quarters, I sat at one end of the bench, the coach and his small son at the other.

Finally, late in the game, with the score tied, the coach beckoned me. Scrambling to his end of the bench, with visions of Frank Ramsey flashing in my mind, I kneeled at the coach's side.

"Reed," said the coach, his face wrinkled in a frown and his eyes fixed on the action on the floor.

"Yeah, coach? Yeah? Yeah?"

"Reed, my son has to go to the bathroom. Take him downstairs, will ya?"

Well, Kindred has written a book that is universal in its appeal, one that Frank Ramsey should enjoy as much as an old Park Methodist Bluejay. It's so full of fact and love that it's as if he were a native Kentuckian. Come to think of it, Kindred — like Adolph Rupp — has been with us so long that he IS a Kentuckian, through and through. And at the risk of sounding corny, I've got to observe that Illinois' loss has been a wonderful blessing for all of us who love to read about basketball almost as much as we love to watch it.

Billy Reed

For Cheryl and Jeff

"Basketball is truly a 'dream game' for our entire country. I used to think it was just Indiana, then Illinois and Kentucky, but now it is truly nationwide.

John Wooden, in a letter to the author, July, 1975

Much of the material in this book appeared in one form or another in *The Courier-Journal* and *The Louisville Times* over the last thirty years. I've borrowed anecdotes, facts and ideas from staff writers Larry Boeck, Johnny Carrico, Earl Cox, Joe Creason, Denny Dressman, Dean Eagle, Dick Fenlon, Tommy Fitzgerald, John Flynn, Gerald Griffith, John Ed Pearce, Billy Reed, Gary Schultz, Jim Terhune and Bob White.

Billy Thompson, a sports writer with *The Lexington Herald* when Kelly Coleman was king, was gracious with his help. So were these sports information directors: Russell Rice, at the University of Kentucky; Gary Tuell, Louisville; Ed Given, Western Kentucky; Karl Park, Eastern Kentucky; Fred Hensley, Morehead State and Don Baker, University of Kansas.

Mostly, I want to thank the nice basketball people who put up with my questions, especially Adolph Rupp, who chewed me out a lot, but always ended his scoldings by saying, "Now, what was it you wanted to talk about, young man?"

D. K., October, 1975

"THE GAME IS ALL THE RAGE"

A pair of sweat socks made this book possible. Thank you, sweat socks. Without them, I never would have played basketball, and who knows what I would have done to pass time? Study, maybe? Take piano lessons? Except for the sweat socks, I might be Van Cliburn today or F. Lee Bailey. But the sweat socks made me a basketball player and, ultimately, a sports writer. A sports writer is a basketball player who can type better than he can shoot.

The first I heard of basketball, I wanted nothing to do with it. My third-grade buddies talked about "offense" and "defense." I had no idea what those mysterious words meant, and I certainly wasn't going to ask. So when anyone wondered why I avoided the game, I said, " 'Cause baseball's more fun." Besides ignorance, fear was a factor. The basketball coach was mean. If you made a mistake, he ordered you to run laps around the gym. The monster.

And yet I wound up on the fourth grade team. Even the risk of embarrassment in front of my peers — would I do "offense" when the right thing was "defense"? — couldn't keep me out of those glorious white sweat socks. I turned the tops down over my black shoes in worshipful imitation of the local high school hero. The spats-like look, in a later day, would have caused laughter miles around. But for a corn-town fourth grader in 1951, it was cool, man. A snapshot of me in uniform that year reveals a laughing little whippersnapper whose carefree appearance suggests total command of this simple game called basketball. Amazing what a good pair of sweat socks can do.

From that lowly beginning, I never rose much. Too small, not quick enough, inconsistent shooter. But a helluva typist. So here I am writing a fat book about basketball in Kentucky because a book about my noteworthy accomplishments as a player would be very thin and nobody would buy it except my mother (and she'd want extra S & H stamps).

Well, there *was* the night at Hartsburg. In the first half of a high school game, I scored 16 points. During the halftime break, our coach, Eldridge Carson (Doc) Kinsey Jr., must have spoken to us. It was his custom to remark loudly on our failings. During these harangues, I didn't look the coach in the eye, mainly

1

because I liked to watch his Adam's apple bob up and down over his red bow tie. Kinsey talked around an omnipresent toothpick. He chewed gum, too. In all, his intermission presentations were wonderful theater, full of suspense: Will he take me out of the game? (Please, coach, one more chance.) Will his bow tie, worried so much by its anatomical neighbor, come loose? Can he last the season without swallowing either the gum or the toothpick?

This night at Hartsburg, I had no time for conjecture. I spent the entire break figuring up how many points I would score by game's end. Let's see — two times 16 is 32 . . . 16 + 16 equals 32 . . . 16 + 8 + 8 (to break my future scoring down into quarters) is also 32. Another Cousy!

Only trouble was, Hartsburg noticed that the little guy wearing glasses was throwing them in from his socks. So they made an elementary defensive change. The man guarding me simply moved a step to my right. That wouldn't bother a good offensive player. It drove me flat crazy. If I wanted to shoot, I then had to go to my left. Oh, how I wanted to shoot! Only four points, four points only, would give me 20 for the first time ever. The cheerleaders would like that. (True confession: Even more than turned-down socks, I liked cheerleaders and played every game hoping they'd notice me — and wondering what to do if they did.) Alas. Not yet able to go to my left, I scored one point the second half.

End of semi-noteworthy accomplishment.

I've often wondered why so many people invest so much time watching a kid's game. Why do they care so deeply what happens? At its highest levels, bas-

ketball demands grace and speed, strength and agility. The perfect basketball game is a ballet of war. The next time you see good players on television, turn off the sound. Let them glide and fly and sail in silence. Nureyev couldn't carry Dr. J's sweat socks. To this beauty, add tests of will and simple muscular power — a George McGinnis who wants to slam-dunk over an Artis Gilmore — and no game is basketball's match.

But that is not why people care; that is a bonus. Only a few marvels of nature — Elgin Baylor and Rick Barry and David Thompson, to name three — are on those terms with the game. The rest of us are 5 feet 7 with anvil feet and hands like catchers' mitts. And *that* is why we care. These deficiencies are mere inconveniences, for if melancholy reality settles in (can't go to your left?), we still have our dreams, our long-ago dreams. At a basketball game, for a few shining moments, we are kids again, having fun, unencumbered by taxes and bill collectors. The crabgrass can wait another day. The world is 94 feet long, 50 feet wide, and there's a hoop at each end. What Jim Naismith did in 1891 was invent a dream machine. He only called it basketball.

Naismith was a Canadian who left the ministry at age 29 to enroll in a YMCA training school at Springfield, Massachusetts. The winter of '91, he was put in charge of a quarrelsome crowd of physical education students with orders to keep them out of trouble until the snow melted. Played by the rules, lacrosse, soccer, rugby and football were invitations to mayhem in the tiny YMCA gymnasium. And Naismith's modifications of the rules, designed to produce gentility, moved the "incorrigibles," as they were

Dr. James Naismith with the original equipment used in his new game of basketball — a soccer ball and two peach baskets.

NAISMITH'S ORIGINAL RULES

Completed on Jan. 15, 1892 — first rules made in December, 1891.

1. The ball may be thrown in any direction with one or both hands.

2. The ball may be batted in any direction with one or both hands, (never with the fist).

3. A player cannot run with the ball. The player must throw it from the spot on which he catches it, allowance to be made for a man who catches the ball when running at a good speed if he tries to stop.

4. The ball must be held in or between the hands. The arms or body must not be used for holding it.

5. No shouldering, holding, pushing, tripping or striking in any way the person of an opponent shall be allowed; the first infringement of this rule by any player shall count as a foul, the second shall disqualify the person for the whole of the game, no substitute allowed.

6. A foul is striking at the ball with the fist, violation of Rules 3, 4, and such as described in Rule 5.

7. If either side makes three consecutive fouls, it shall count a goal for the opponents. (Consecutive means without the opponents in the meantime making a foul.)

8. A goal shall be made when the ball is thrown or batted from the grounds into the basket and stays there, providing those defending the goal do not touch or disturb the goal. If the ball rests on the edges and the opponent moves the basket, it shall count as a goal.

9. When the ball goes out of bounds, it shall be thrown into the field of play by the person first touching it. In case of a dispute, the umpire shall call a foul on that side.

10. The umpire shall be judge of the men and shall note the fouls and notify the referee when three consecutive fouls have been made. He shall have power to

11. The referee shall be judge of the ball and shall decide when the ball is in play, in bounds, and to which side it belongs, and shall keep time. He shall decide when a goal has been made and keep account of the goals, with any other duties that are usually performed by a referee.

12. The time shall be two fifteen minute halves, with five minute rest between.

13. The side making the most goals in that time shall be declared the winner. In case of a draw, the game may, by agreement of the captains, be continued until another goal is made.

The goals are a couple of baskets or boxes about fifteen inches in diameter across the opening, and about fifteen inches deep. These are suspended, one at each end of the grounds, about ten feet from the floor. The object of the game is to put the ball into your opponent's goal. This may be done by throwing the ball from any part of the grounds, with one or both hands . . .

The number composing a team depends largely on the size of the floor space, but it may range from three on a side to forty. The fewer players down to three, the more scientific it may be made but the more players, the more fun. The men may be arranged according to the idea of the captain, but it has been found that a goal keeper, two guards, three center men, two wings, and a home man stationed in the above order from the goal is the best.

It shall be the duty of the goal keeper and the two guards to prevent the opponent from scoring. The duty of the wing man and the home man is to put the ball into the opponent's goal, and the center man shall feed the ball forward to the man who has the best opportunity; thus nine men make the best number for a team.

We would advise the director to keep a good firm grasp on the ruling for awhile called, to giggling fits.

Naismith needed a new game. The YMCA gym was only 65 feet long. That made running with a ball impractical. Besides, how would a runner be stopped if not with a tackle? The night before his last class with the incorrigibles, Naismith sat in his little office above the locker room. Suddenly, it came to him. "If he can't run with the ball, we don't have to tackle," Naismith said aloud. "And if we don't have to tackle, the roughness will be eliminated. I've got it!"

Once set with the fundamental rules of no running and no tackling, Naismith moved quickly. A soccer ball would be the perfect size for passing about. Scoring would be accomplished by tossing the ball into a goal. He considered a lacrosse-type goal but discarded it because it is a vertical target. As such, it would encourage hard throwing and, given the incorrigibles' habits, set off World War I. The goal needed to be horizontal to produce an arched, gentle toss.

The next morning, Naismith asked the YMCA janitor, Mr. Stebbins, for two wooden boxes about 18 inches square. Stebbins had none, but he said, "I have two old peach baskets down in the storeroom if they'll do you any good." It was a day in December of 1891, perhaps Dec. 21, when the YMCA rowdies played the first basketball game ever. There were nine men to a side. The final score was 1-0. The goal was made by William R. Chase from almost mid-court (25 feet). Janitor Stebbins, on a ladder, retrieved the ball from a peach basket nailed to the gymnasium balcony. Hoop hysteria, pardon the expression, was born.

It spread quickly. Thanks mainly to the YMCA's national organization, basketball was everywhere within a year. The YMCA *Review* of Herkimer, New York, asked, "Gone Crazy! Who?" The newspaper answered: "Ministers, lawyers, bankers, editors, merchants, clerks, mechanics, boys, young men, older men, yes, everybody plays basketball now." Providence, Rhode Island, reported "basketball fever is contagious." Salem, Oregon, said "the game is all the rage."

In the summer Sioux Indians played basketball on their reservation in South Dakota — only 16 years after Custer couldn't get the ball upcourt against Sitting Bull's press. The Sioux made goal supports of small saplings and put up baskets that were rings of bent willow branches.

A homemade goal. Yes, Jim Naismith did all right. My first goal was a net-less rim nailed over the doorway of a tool shed. It is distinguished in memory by the damage it did my head.

The rim was about nine feet from the ground, a foot below regulation. (But then, I was 14 years old and about five feet, two inches tall, which is less than regulation, too.) Just as giants like Wilt Chamberlain itch to shoot from 20 feet out, so do little guys wearing glasses want to do the impossible. More than anything, I wanted to dunk the cussed ball. Just once, Lord. Let me dunk it and I'll brush my teeth every day forever. Just once, and then I'll be little again. Alas. Not even a heavenly compact made the impossible possible. I just couldn't do it, not even on my nine-foot rim.

Wait! How about if I stood on the doorway step? It was a foot up. Then I could leap from the step and dunk it. Why hadn't I thought of this before? So I crouched in the doorway. And I sprang mightily upward.

Yes.

I crashed my head into the top of the doorway frame.

I fell to the ground, dazed, not knowing what had happened. I never tried that again.

My father, a carpenter, soon built a goal. It was a treasure, 10 feet high, an elaborate collection of 2-by-4's and plywood left over from his jobs. What more could a kid ask? Growing up in a corn town of 1,300 people, a boy needed nothing beyond a basketball and a goal. With those, he needed no movies, no television, no radio, no beaches, no dances. With those, he could work a magic all his own.

I wasn't much of a player. They called me a playmaker, which didn't fool me even at the time. A playmaker is a little guy wearing glasses who can't shoot and isn't smart enough to dunk one without half-killing himself. I wasn't much — except in those hours alone at my goal, there in the dust (for the grass wore out quickly) and in the mud (the ball bounced funny). Then, by the lovely power of imagination, I became Don Ohl of Illinois. Ohl was a guard, a beautiful shooter. I saw him on television. He had a way of releasing the ball with both hands in an action so smooth and gentle you'd think he was lifting a small bird to its first flight. If I were a sorry Robin Freeman of Ohio State (his unstoppable jumper, shot from behind his head, always wound up in my mother's tomatoes), some days I was a terrific Don Ohl. The day at McLean: I went to a gym in a little town three miles up US 66. For two hours, shooting alone, I did not miss a shot from anywhere. Not a single one. Well, maybe one, but not two. It was phantasmagorical. An old man came over when I finished, and he said, "What is your name?" I told him, and I went home — to dream, dream, dream. Even today, 17 or 18 years later, only writing about it, I feel a sensational tingling in my hands. Give me the ball. Set a pick, somebody. I can shoot! (Going to my right.)

Because perhaps 20 million people play basketball in over 130 countries with eight zillion crazies cheering them on, no claim is laid to Kentucky having the best players or the most ardent fans. It is enough to say that basketball is special in Kentucky. And it is, for if they play the game best in the big cities, as they surely do, it is in the small towns they love it most. Small towns like Atlanta, Illinois, and Cynthiana, Kentucky.

Joe Hall, the University of Kentucky basketball coach, grew up in Cynthiana. "As a kid, I'd listen to Kentucky on the radio at the kitchen table, and I'd keep score myself. I remember reading that Wah Jones (a remarkable Kentucky player) drank milk every day. That really impressed me. I love Kentucky basketball."

In a state populated by fewer than three and a half million people — and nearly a third of those in three large metropolitan areas — Hall's job took him to a hundred Cynthianas. "People throughout this state really care about basketball," he said. "Businessmen tell me that business goes up and down, depending on whether we win or not. When we lose, a little bit of those people dies."

They care about basketball in Kentucky. You can curse the bourbon they make; pass the Scotch, please. If country ham upsets your nervous system with its thirsty demand for a gallon of water after breakfast, then no one will care much if you go for sausage instead. You can

Basketball was immediately popular with Kentuckians. This team won the YMCA championship in Louisville in 1895, only four years after the sport was invented in Massachusetts.

ignore horse racing, too, passing it off as a rich man's hobby and a poor man's disease. Do all that if you want. You will get by. But to live in peace in Kentucky, you should have mastered the reverse pivot by age 9.

With its small, rural towns, none with much money, Kentucky came naturally by basketball, a simple game that could be played by any kid with a ball, a hoop and a dream. Pick names from a map, and they play the game there: Ashland, Paintsville, Inez and Betsy Layne . . . Wayland, Pikeville, Virgie, Hazard, Hindman and Carr Creek . . . Hazel Green, Morehead, Londin, Corbin and Lawrenceburg (where a brilliant teacher named Rhoda Kavanaugh started her own school and attended basketball games with an umbrella in hand should a player need extra coaxing). . . . Irvine, Maysville and Richmond . . . Covington and Corinth, Paris and Somerset, Lexington and Moreland . . . Burnside, Campbellsville and Munfordville . . . Hartford, Hardinsburg, Scottsville, Central City, Earlington and Owensboro (where Kentucky Wesleyan won four NCAA college-division championships, leading fans to call it "the little UCLA"). . . . Dawson Springs and Murray, Brewers and Cuba, Benton, Lone Oak and Monkey's Eyebrow (where Doris Duley, who runs the nearby Fin 'n' Feather restaurant, put up a goal for her 10-year-old daughter, Terri). At Balltown, the man behind the counter at Bryant's Grocery said, "Naw, wasn't named for basketball far as I know. A family named Ball settled here. The town's about 150 years old, and I don't think basketball was that important back then."

Joe Begley and his wife run a general store along KY 7 in Letcher County in the mountains of Eastern Kentucky. A philosopher of sorts, Begley is a fierce opponent of strip-mining for coal. In the '30's he played on a Maytown High School team that made it to the State Tournament. I asked him once what he thought about basketball in Kentucky, and Joe Begley said, "If a lump of coal ain't Jesus Christ, basketball is." He smiled at that one.

"LOOK WHERE THEY'RE PLAYING THAT GAME"

James Naismith played in only two basketball games. "Just didn't get around to playing," he said. With six other Springfield YMCA instructors, he played against seven students March 11, 1892, in the first public game ever. The students won, 5-1, the instructors being saved from total humiliation by a short, stocky young man named Amos Alonzo Stagg, who dressed in his old Yale football uniform and played with such passion that he acquired a black eye. "I wish Lonnie could have made that point without fouling everybody," Naismith said to a reporter from *The Springfield Republican.* Not that the burly, walrus-mustached Naismith was innocent. With a background of wrestling, boxing and football, he too used tactics that he intended to keep out of his new game. "Once I even used a grapevine wrestling clamp on a man who was too big for me to handle," the Father of Basketball confessed.

More than 150 million people pay to see basketball games in the United States each year. Kentucky accounts for maybe three million customers. Just as Naismith would tremble in agitation should he see a basketball game today

with its incessant physical contact, so would he grumble at the sport's commercialization. "He thought it should have been only a playground activity," said one of his daughters, Mrs. Helen Dodd of Westcliffe, Colorado. "He didn't totally approve of it as an intercollegiate sport . . . and he would have been appalled by the present emphasis on professional basketball."

Naismith liked his game the way he dreamed of it. Mrs. Dodd said, "He started collecting pictures of some of the odd places in which he would find baskets: In alleys, farm yards, and gosh knows where else. He would get quite a chuckle out of those pictures, and he almost always would say, 'Look where they're playing that game.'"

Goals are everywhere in Kentucky. Customers at a grocery store on the Mountain Parkway can shoot 30-footers from the bread shelves. At Red Fox, a gas station best serves its clients during time-outs. At Jackson, a funeral home has a hoop next to the hearse's parking spot.

A goal need not be storebought. A clothes basket, with the bottom still in it, is tacked to an abandoned church near

Hazard. Not far from Monkey's Eyebrow, a bicycle tire rim (with the spokes removed) is the accomplice of a boy's imagination.

New nets, no nets, ripped nets, nets of chain, nets of clothesline rope, red-white-and-blue nets, just plain nets. Nailed to trees, telephone poles, garages, work-sheds, great white mansions (Joe Gregory, the first owner of the pro Kentucky Colonels, built a gym next to his place. Ellie and John Y. Brown, later owners of the Colonels, have a basket over their three-car garage.) Whether grafted onto

Vine Grove

a dog house in Hardinsburg or attached to a housewife's clothesline pole outside Mayfield; no matter if the rim is a re-worked clothes hanger like one outside Balltown or if the backboard is corrugated tin like one in Elizabethtown; whether the shooter has to stand on the railroad tracks in Burnaugh or in the street in Wurtland — no matter what, they all are basketball goals, and in the end they all are the same as the one Terry Lee Thomas built outside Vine Grove when he was 14.

Terry Lee and a neighbor boy, Tom

Near Monkey's Eyebrow

Leslie County

Phillips, went over to Gilbert Young's land to cut down two trees to use as supports for the backboard and rim. They used axes, and it took them a day to cut down and trim the trees. They carried them, one at a time, the half-mile to home. Using a posthole digger, they made holes four feet deep in an open lot between the boys' houses.

They made the backboard from 3/4-inch plywood that Terry Lee's brother, Dicky, didn't use in his new house in Louisville. They bought a rim at Jones' Variety Store in Vine Grove, paying $2.98,

Jefferson County

Fulton County

and attached it to the plywood with screws. After the goal had been up six months, the boys didn't use it much. The ground in front turned to mud a lot. Another thing was that the rim was 12 feet high, two feet higher than Jim Naismith suggested. "We messed up, I guess," Terry Lee Thomas said.

"Look where they're playing that game," Naismith said. In Kentucky, they play basketball in places you've never seen. Places like. . . .

Marshall County

Randy Price, Turners Station

TURNERS STATION, January, 1975 —The blacktop road between Campbellsburg and Turners Station runs alongside a twisting creek and some railroad tracks. There's not much traffic. So Randy Price, who is 13 years old, dribbled his basketball down the righthand lane, going home before dark.

About 3:30 in the afternoon that day, Randy figured he'd go rabbit hunting with his friend up the road, Patrick Dooley. It was a fine day, bright as could be. Against the winter chill, Randy threw on a couple of sweatshirts, old blue jeans, a couple pair of socks and his knee-high hunting boots. He pulled his knit cap down to his eyebrows.

Most likely, any mother would be pleased to call Randy hers. He's sturdy, maybe 5 feet 6 and 120 pounds. His eyes are brown and they laugh a lot, and his nose, a broad one, turns up at every smile. Ever so faintly, freckles decorate his cheeks.

"I was goin' huntin', but then I thought not," Randy said. "I'd just play basketball."

It's about half a mile between the Price place and Dooley's. Patrick walked over and the two buddies shot for a while at the goal on the garage by Randy's house. Then they went to see if they could fix the net on Patrick's basket.

"Wasn't anything we could do," Randy said. "It just got wet, I figure, and got rotten, and when Patrick put a shot through it, it just ripped up. Really don't matter. That net wasn't no count to begin with."

Winter-brown pastures by the blacktop road faded with nightfall. Walking in the mud at the roadside, Randy kept his basketball on the blacktop by bouncing it left-handed. Cattle on hilltops stood on

the day's last, thin, redding sunbeams. Randy carried the ball now and then, cradling it under his arm, against his hip, going home before dark to shoot a little more.

Turners Station is a tiny collection of houses out in the country. It's in Henry County, about 15 miles from Carrollton. Until four years ago, the Prices lived "right in the middle of Turners Station, five houses down from my grandmother's," Randy said. Now they've moved a mile or two outside town into a nice brick house.

They took along the basketball goal. "It was my dad's, too," Randy said. "I helped him put it up here about a year ago." Attached to the garage, the goal is about 8-1/2 feet off the ground. "I haven't dunked one yet, but I keep on tryin'," Randy said.

He shoots there a lot. "Every day in the summer. And at night. We turn on that light inside the garage." Randy's father, Harold, who works at the aluminum plant in Carrollton, played high school ball at Campbellsburg. "He's got a bad back now, though. He had to work too much when he was young. He worked

every day. His dad had about 11 children, and only half of 'em would work."

When Patrick Dooley comes over, Randy plays "Horse," "Twenty-one" and "Around the world," all shooting games. In "world," as Randy calls it, the first shot is from the little hole in the driveway, about six feet out. The longest shot is from behind the second hump, 20 feet away.

"We play a lot," Randy said. "There's nothin' to do in Turners Station, 'cept shoot. We put up a basket at my grandmother's house, too."

A man passing through Turners Station challenged Randy to a game of "world." It was fun, after years, to shoot a muddy basketball, to feel again the dirt caking on his fingertips. A bad shot bounced off the rim and rolled down a hill into a little creek. "That's why I'm wearin' these boots," Randy said.

Later, with the sun gone, the man drove away. Randy waved, holding the basketball under his left arm, against his hip.

ST. JOSEPH, February, 1970 — "Over here," said Father Walter Hancock, "we have the smallest gym in the United

St. Alphonsus gym.

States." Father Hancock is the priest at St. Alphonsus Church in St. Joseph, about 10 miles outside Owensboro. He's also principal and basketball coach of St. Alphonsus Grade School. "This is our furnace house," he said, pointing to a building which had only its roof above ground level. "When we changed from coal to gas, that left us enough room in there to build the gym."

The gym is no more than 20 feet long. It is 10 feet wide. Steam pipes pass through open space seven feet off the floor. Two baskets are hooked to the wall, one directly over the only door, one on the other side of the pipes. With concrete-block walls and floor, with two bare light bulbs making eerie shadows, the place looks less a gym and more a cell for the solitary confinement of a basketball player.

St. Alphonsus practices there when it's too cold to practice outside (on a paved court with six baskets, built with $1,200 raised by Fr. Hancock, who says with a smile, "They call me Father Black-top here.") About five or six boys fit comfortably into the gym, but the coach-priest-fund raiser insists he can squeeze in 10 for dribbling practice if they don't move around too much. They play their games in West Louisville, paying $20 to rent a gym. It is important, Fr. Hancock said, for a small grade school such as his — 111 students, 50 of them boys — to play basketball. "It helps out the kids," he said. "It gives them coordination, helps them to think and teaches them to obey rules. Basketball players make better grades."

EDDYVILLE, February, 1970 — Everett Cherry stopped one of his players. "Basketball is big here, isn't it?"

Eddyville State Penitentiary

Prisoner No. 26787 smiled. "Only thing fit to do here."

Cherry is the recreation director at Kentucky State Penitentiary at Eddyville. His intramural basketball program includes 10 teams of 12 players each. He also has a varsity team, called the Penitentiary Roadrunners. Basketball is big at Eddyville.

When the Roadrunners play — always at home, by the way, either in the Western Kentucky Independent League, or against, say, one of the college fraternity teams that always ask for games — about 500 of the prison's 1,000 inmates come to watch.

They cheer for the outside team. "It's a funny thing," Cherry said. "I guess it's their way of showing their gratitude to the outsiders who come here to play."

The basketball, Cherry said, is good. "We had a boy who was so good — well, Larry Conley and Larry Pursiful from the University of Kentucky played against him one time, and he beat them to death. He scored 52 points and got 29 rebounds. We won 148-142. I think 74 was the highest he ever scored. He was good for 40 every time."

Where is he now?

"In jail in Lexington, last I heard."

Any chance of getting him back with the Roadrunners?

"I hate to wish it on anybody that he should wind up in Eddyville. But if he has to go to prison again, I hope it's here."

Basketball is good for the prisoners, Cherry said. Somebody asked him, only half-jokingly, if his players ever tried to escape with the team from the outside. Cherry said, "The inmates who play basketball are all tired out from playing. They're thinking about basketball. They don't go around planning things."

Besides, Cherry said, the basketball players are a "higher type" people than the typical inmate. "I'm not saying they aren't the low class when they start, but they come out of that low class fast. The boys in basketball don't have anything to do with the low morals of penitentiary life, the robbing and beating. You don't find basketball boys with home-made daggers or pipes, that sort of stuff."

HELL FOR CERTAIN, March, 1974 — To go to Hell for Certain, you turn left off KY 257. That puts you on a dirt road next to Hell for Certain Creek. Drive on it two and a half miles. When you see a young man fishing, stop the car.

The boy's name is Boone Hall. He's 12 years old. To do his fishing, he sometimes sits on a wooden bridge by that dirt road. Across the bridge is the Hell for Certain Community Center. You should ask Boone Hall if anyone plays basketball there. He'll say, "Me."

Hell for Certain is no major metropolitan center. It is a mountain community of 70 or 80 people who live along nine miles of the creek in Southeastern Kentucky. The nearest town is Hyden, 10 miles south. Driving on that dirt road barely wide enough for a car, you worry a lot. Going through mudholes, you wonder what will happen should you get stuck. Clearly, you are going through...

"Yeah, that's how this place got it's name," said Amos Osborne, who grew up here when the only way in and out was by horse or on foot. "Two boys from somewhere else walked clear back here, over the rocks, climbing hills, wading up the creek bed. And one guy said, 'This is sure hell.'

"And the other guy said, 'That's for certain.'"

Osborne's son, Ricky, 15, plays for the Hell for Certain community basketball team. It had a game the other night. "We went over to Wooton, on the other side of Hyden," Ricky said. "They've got a church team there. They beat us 44 to 58."

"I thought it was 8 to 25," fisherman Boone Hall said.

"We got only eight players and Wooton's got 25, is what it is," Ricky said.

He wore a gray T-shirt bearing the words: "Hell Fer Sartin Creek." Ricky bought the shirt at Elam's Department Store in Hyden.

"We're going to play Wooton again," he said.

At Hell for Certain this time?

"Nope, over there again. They've got a school to play at. That's one reason they beat us. They practice there all the time. We're not used to playing in that big a place."

Ricky Osborne spoke in understatement. The Hell for Certain Community Center, only a month old, was built by the people of the community. The mother of the preacher woman at Hell for Certain's church gave them money for materials. The building is made of concrete blocks. Inside are two pool tables, a ping-pong table, a record player — and, yes, a basketball court.

In all of Eastern Kentucky, where basketball is at least majestic if not divine, no gymnasium is the match of Hell for Certain's. Here is no pleasure palace, no waste of the taxpayers' money. This is basic. Henry David Thoreau urged the world to "simplify, simplify." He would have loved Hell for Certain's basketball court.

It's small. The floor is concrete. You know you're out of bounds when you hit a wall. The lighting comes from four bulbs, two on each side of the court.

Instead of setting the baskets at the regulation height of 10 feet, Hell for Certain has them at about eight feet. Otherwise, the rafters would get in the way. The court is 35 feet long, 25 feet wide. Come Sunday afternoon, when church is out, Hell for Certain is the place to be.

"Be so many people playing ball you can't move," said Phillip Hoskins, 22, a coal-truck driver who is a son-in-law of Amos Osborne. It was Amos who donated a half acre of land for the building. He's

Hell for Certain Community Center

an old Hell for Certain boy. His father, a farmer on land no more than a quarter-mile from the new center, died when Amos was 3. Amos left here at age 14 to find work in Indianapolis. He's been back now for 10 years.

For Amos Osborne, who is perhaps 40 years old, Hell for Certain is heaven for sure. It is home. He is proud of it. "You ought to see it here when it snows," he said. "You know those snow pictures, like they use in those cigarette advertisements? They're nowhere near as pretty as it gets here."

The community center, with its basketball court, is Osborne's delight. "Everybody ought to have a center like this," he said. "There wouldn't be much of this stuff going on, this shooting and stealing." Posted on a wall in the building is a sign: "No Drinking...No Fighting... No Gambling." On another wall: "No Rock 'n' Roll Music." To qualify for a key to the center, a person living on Hell for Certain Creek must attend the community church two Sundays every month.

Why is there basketball in Hell for Certain?

"I don't know," Osborne said. "Just natural, I guess."

The basketball court takes up a lot of room, more than half the building. Did the builders ever think about leaving it out?

"Nope. The kids love it."

KINGDOM COME, February, 1968 —Driving down KY 463, you pass through Delphia, which isn't much more than the "Delphia U-Wash Laundry" on the right. Over a hill and you're in Letcher County in the mountains of Southeastern Kentucky, 225 miles from Louisville. At a sign that says "Cumberland 5 miles, Hot Spot 15 miles," you turn left and go down a narrow road four miles — past Dollie's Place, which is a cafe with good hamburgers and a six-foot pool table — and you have found Kingdom Come High School.

It's a sandstone building, three stories high, built in 1925 and named Kingdom Come after the book, *The Little Shepherd of Kingdom Come*, which they say is about this area.

Some 80 kids are in school, and most of them were upstairs the other night for a game with Red Bird High School.

Yes, upstairs. The gymnasium is on the third floor. From one end to the other, the gym is 61 feet long, but the builders left a foot and a half at each end for out-of-bounds room. So the playing court is 58 feet long instead of the regulation 84 feet. This year they put big cushioned mats on the brick chimneys where the baskets are attached. Junior Halcomb, a Kingdom Come player, said "One time, ah liked to busted mah brines out agin' that chimney comin' in for a layup."

The court is 30 feet wide, which is 20 feet less than regulation. The out-of-bounds line on one side is painted against the wall. You're out of bounds if you go through the door in the corner.

On the other side, where there are three rows of bleachers for the fans, people's feet hang onto the court. Not that it matters much. Basketball in Appalachia is informal. During pre-game warm-ups the other night, a Kingdom Come player had to wrestle a fan for the basketball. Given half a chance, the fans shoot baskets. So do the referees. The "B" team boys, who sit on the bench for the varsity game because there are only five varsity

Kingdom Come High School

players, eat popcorn and drink pop during the game.

The action is sometimes strange. The basket rims are too high by maybe six inches. The old wooden floor, which dips and winds as much as KY 463, has spots where the ball just won't bounce. When somebody asked Junior Halcomb what it's like to play at Kingdom Come, he said, "It's hail, man."

Yet Junior is in his junior year and doesn't intend to follow the example of his coach, Jerry Coots, 22, who played half his freshman year at Kingdom Come and then moved to Whitesburg High, the city school. "Ah wouldn't be able to play ball over there," Junior said.

Playing ball means something to him. He has nine brothers and sisters, just one younger than him. Besides shooting pool (he likes the eight-foot table at Mary Jane's Grille across from the school, even though they use rolled-up napkins to support the cushioned rails), Junior said there isn't much to do in the narrow valley that holds Line Fork Creek.

"During the summer, when it's up aroun' a hundred-and-somethin', Ah'm

Cheers for Kingdom Come

in this gym shootin' baskets for five hours and more," Junior said. He is Kingdom Come's leading scorer. He gets about 23 points a game, mostly on his set shot from mid-court.

Kingdom Come doesn't have a good team. It has lost all 12 of its games and is last in *The Courier-Journal's* Litkenhous Ratings of the state's 350 high school teams. It has an 0.1 rating.

Coach Coots, who is called "Coots" by everyone in school, says Kingdom Come has problems it likely will never overcome. Only 30 percent of the fathers in the valley have jobs, he said. Boys leave school to join the Army. They go to Cincinnati or Detroit to work.

"These kids have been losing for so long, they're used to it," Coots said. "They joke it up just as big if they lose as if they'd just won a game."

Maybe.

When Red Bird moved ahead 70-68 and was holding the ball until the final seconds ticked off on an electric alarm clock (the scoreboard had shorted out), a Kingdom Come senior named Sharon Gentry shouted at a Red Bird fan:

"Don't you sound off about winning,

or I'll come down and scratch your eyes out."

And when Junior Halcomb left the floor, after missing two late free throws that would have tied the game, the tears in his eyes were not from joking it up.

CINDERELLA IN SNEAKERS

I tried to find out when the first basketball game was played in Kentucky. It would be impressive, even scholarly, to say the game reached Kentucky on Nov. 19, 1892, when a young Kansan named Adolph Rupp nailed up a bourbon barrel and threw a Hereford into it. I found nothing of the sort (possibly because Rupp wasn't born until 1901). History freaks who pick up this book will need to be satisfied with the one date I consider important and memorable in the love affair Kentucky has with basketball. On March 18, 1928, the Carr Creek High School team lost to Ashland 13-11 in four overtime periods in a game at Lexington for the state championship. Carr Creek was Cinderella in sneakers, and whenever romantics speak of small-town teams like Tolu and Heath, Corinth and Sharpe, Cuba and Brewers and Inez — all those ragged urchins who won our hearts — we can never forget the Creekers.

In '28 Carr Creek was a community of maybe 200 people. The school sat on a ledge carved out of the side of a mountain in Knott County. Of 15 students in high school, eight were boys.

Mules pulling shovels dug out a level place for the boys to play basketball. One goal was on a chicken shed, the other on a railroad tie. Ellis Johnson, a star player for Ashland in '28 and later an All-America at Kentucky and a successful college coach, once said he knew why the Carr Creek players handled the ball so well. "The sides of their outdoor court dropped off a hill maybe 75 to 100 feet down. If a kid threw a ball away or fumbled it, he had a long climb. That pretty much discouraged careless passes."

Carr Creek had no gymnasium. There was an auditorium. "That's where we had chapel every day, reading the Bible and all," said Gurney Adams, a guard on the '28 Creekers. "We had baskets in there, in case it rained or snowed outdoors. Only trouble was, the durned ceiling wasn't but 12 feet high. You couldn't put much arch on a shot." For games, Carr Creek traveled by mule-drawn log wagon as far as the dirt roads went. They then proceeded by foot over the mountains, maybe five or six miles. It was an event of everlasting moment when the Creekers caught a train to Hazard, 20 miles away, and stayed overnight in a hotel.

23

The 1928 Creekers were not sartorial wonders.

Carr Creek High School

They had no basketball uniforms. Legend says the mountain men played in bib overalls, which sounds quaint enough, but another report has them wearing white undershirts and khaki pants. The team's coach was Oscar Morgan, a grade-school teacher whose basketball credentials consisted of attendance at a few games while studying at Centre College.

Through the semifinals of the 1928 regional tournament at Richmond, Carr Creek had won 14 games without a defeat and their run-run-run style of play, both on offense and in a man-to-man pressing

1928
National Champions

Ashland High of '28 had real warmup suits.

defense, so captivated the people of Richmond that they pitched in to buy the Creekers real uniforms, at a cost of $55, for the championship game. Victory there sent Carr Creek into the State Tournament at Lexington.

The tournament then was in its 11th year. Lexington and Louisville schools had won nine of the first 10 championships, and in '28 the favorites were Louisville St. Xavier, Lawrenceburg and Ashland. Carr Creek was a curiosity, not a contender. That changed quickly enough, for the Creekers promptly dis-

patched their first three opponents by scores of 31-11, 21-11, and 37-11. Meanwhile, Ashland, also undefeated, won 16-8, 25-13 and 22-13.

The night of March 18, 1928, came up foul. It snowed and sleeted. Yet more than 4,000 customers stuffed the University of Kentucky's 3,500-seat Alumni Gym for the state championship game. Carr Creek led at half-time by the score of 4-3, which was unusually low even in those days of the center jump. The lack of scoring was attributed to Ashland's zone defense and Carr Creek's man-to-man

Ellis Johnson of Ashland, All-State, All-America

press. Neither team had gone up against the like before.

Ashland moved to a 9-6 lead early in the fourth quarter. But with three minutes left, Gillis Madden sank a long shot for Carr Creek. Then, with 30 seconds to go, Shelby Stamper's free throw tied the game 9-9. Through three overtime periods, neither team scored.

Ashland took an 11-9 lead early in the fourth overtime on Gene Strothers' layup. Unable to penetrate Ashland's zone and growing desperate, Carr Creek missed a long shot. Then Ashland's Ellis

Johnson began killing the clock by dribbling from one end of the floor to the other (there was no midcourt line then). Eventually Johnson worked loose for a layup and Ashland led 13-9. Carr Creek retained a measure of hope when Stamper made a long shot with a minute to play, but Ashland controlled the subsequent tip and Johnson dribbled away the time.

Forty-six years later, a visitor to Carr Creek asked Gurney Adams about that defeat. "It was rough," Adams said. He twisted up his face, scowling at the sour memory. "I'd have liked to play 'em

When the mountain teams were king. Hazard High won the state championship in 1932. Coach Pat Payne is at the right in the back row. One of his players, Morton Combs, second from right in the front row, later coached Carr Creek to the 1956 state championship.

again up there in Chicago."

The Creekers visited the Windy City. Cinderella went Big Time. Both Ashland and Carr Creek were invited to a national high school tournament at the University of Chicago. The Creekers had taken their first train ride out of Kentucky, and now they were to see a moving box called an elevator. In the 40-team tournament they quickly became the favorite of the crowd, which included a young Illinois high school coach named Adolph Rupp.

Carr Creek won its first two games. It beat the U.S. Indian School of Albuquerque, New Mexico, 32-16, and then defeated Austin, Texas, 25-18. Another victory would have produced a rematch with Ashland, but the Creekers lost to Vienna, Georgia, 22-11. Ashland went on to win the tournament, finishing the season undefeated in 37 games.

Basketball in the mountains of Eastern Kentucky, basketball as Carr Creek played it, once was the standard of excellence for the state. In the 17 state tournaments from 1940 to 1956, mountain schools won seven championships: Hazel Green in '40, Inez in '41 and '54, Hindman in '43, Harlan in '44, Hazard in '55 and

Carr Creek in '56.

But in the 19 state tournaments following Carr Creek's victory, not a single mountain school even made it to the championship game. Louisville schools won 11 championships in that time and finished second six times.

"I have a theory on that," said R. B. Singleton, once a player at Carr Creek and principal there when the school closed down in 1974. "People say the kids nowadays have other things to do. Cars and that. But, really, around Carr Creek, there's *nothing* — except basketball.

"My theory is that we were ahead of our time back then. We had kids playing basketball in the fifth grade. A feeder system. Well, now Louisville does that, too. And they have so many more kids to choose from."

There are other ideas. Integration, for one. Carr Creek's championship was earned in the last year that Kentucky kept black high schools out of the State Tournament. Once allowed to play, black teams have been dominant. The last all-white team to win was Shelby County in 1966. From 1970 through 1975, the state champions did not have a white player on

Corbin High players at the 1948 State Tournament.

the starting team.

"The day of the small school is over in Kentucky," said Jock Sutherland, a veteran of 20 years in high school coaching. "The black element has changed the game—black quickness, black endurance and the black athlete's ability to be uninhibited.

"Whether anyone wants to admit that or not, it's so. Especially in the metropolitan areas. Outside the metropolitan areas, Kentucky high school basketball is not as strong as it was. But in the cities, it's much stronger than it's ever been."

Soon there will be very few small schools. Consolidation already has reduced the number of Kentucky high schools from over 500 to about 300. Cinderella's time has passed. A man went to Carr Creek in March of 1974 for the school's last basketball game. The next year Carr Creek students attended Knott County Central High.

"It's sad, to know this is the last year," said Dale Combs, whose husband, Morton, coached the '56 Creekers. The Combs' home was a bounce pass away from Carr Creek High.

"Morton's and my whole life has been in that building," she said. "Morton raised money himself to build toilets and to add a home economics department. And the gym — the people built it with their own hands."

Warren Amburgey played on that '56 team. So his son could play where the father's dream came true, Amburgey quit his job of 16 years in Louisville, borrowed money and bought a plumbing business between Hindman and Carr Creek. Donnie Amburgey was Carr Creek's leading scorer in '74.

"Donnie lived down here with his grandparents for his freshman year," Amburgey said. "We thought he'd come back to Louisville — but he never did." The father seemed proud of that.

Amburgey came to Carr Creek every weekend that next year. It's a 460-mile round trip. "I worked the night shift. So I'd look for a job here until Monday noon, then head back to Louisville."

Donnie Amburgey kept his father's scrapbook. "We used to talk about how he played for Carr Creek," he said. "And I wanted to, too."

With 14 seconds to play, and Carr

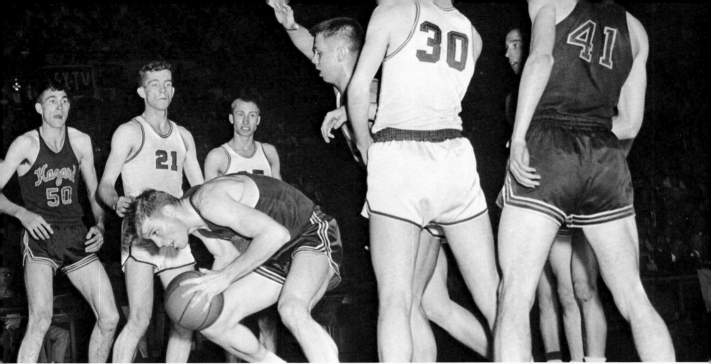

That's Johnny Cox of Hazard at the left.

Creek behind 77-62 in the last game the school would ever play, Dale Combs touched a finger first to her left eye, then to the right, as if wiping away tears.

"I was," the coach's wife said. "I hoped nobody would notice. I sat here thinking, 'No more Carr Creek.'"

Warren Amburgey was in the top row of the bleachers. "It's the end of the Creekers," he said. He spoke softly. "It's hurtful."

Gene Cain (99) of Inez tries to fly in the '46 tournament.

Memories at Carr Creek.

Carr Creek's last basketball game.

KING KELLY, THE ONE AND ONLY

Kelly Coleman scored a record 50 points in the first game of the 1956 State Tournament in Lexington's Memorial Coliseum. The next game he made 39 and, in a semifinal defeat, 28. Following that he scored 68 points in the third-place game. So he averaged 46.3 points a game, which is good for mortals, but for Kelly Coleman it was under his season's average of 46.9. When the third-place game ended, celebrants carried Coleman off the floor (against his wishes). He dressed hurriedly without benefit of a shower, left the Coliseum, hired a taxi and was in a tavern drinking beer (three mugs) during the championship game. He was 17 years old, already a legend: King Kelly Coleman, a coal miner's son, the greatest scorer in Kentucky basketball history, a man-child given to girls, basketball, bragging, beer and trouble (although not necessarily in that order).

Nothing Kelly Coleman ever did, on the court or off, surprised his intimates. Ralph Carlisle said of him, "Gosh almighty, he was just the best." Coleman's coach at Wayland High School, deep in the mountains of Eastern Kentucky, was Copper John Campbell, who said,

"Adolph Rupp told me Kelly was a combination of Alex Groza, Frank Ramsey and Cliff Hagan." Copper John, a diplomat, also said newspapers used too much ink on Coleman. "It made him feel his Cheerios, if you know what I mean."

Coleman came to be called King Kelly when an imaginative sports writer decided coal was no longer king in Eastern Kentucky, that it had been replaced in the hearts of the mountain people by a basketball player whose exploits, even 20 years later, seemed incredible. A dozen times in his senior season, Coleman scored over 50 points. Once he made 75 (and had 41 rebounds the same night).

The mailman in Wayland grew weary toting Kelly's mail that year. Daily he would leave a large canvas bag of letters outside the Coleman's $15-a-month house on the right fork of Beaver Creek. From Utah and California, from Ohio and Indiana, from everywhere people sent Coleman money, a dollar maybe, $5, even $75 once. Girls pursued him, and he often made certain they caught up. King Kelly the student? Some days the high school principal, Lawrence Price, telephoned the Coleman home and asked the player's

mother, "Rusha, is Kelly out of bed yet?" Coleman, from his second-floor bedroom, shouted down, "Tell him I'll be there in time for practice."

As a freshman at Wayland High, Coleman averaged 19 points a game. He raised that to 26 the next year, and he broke the state scoring record his junior season with a 32.6 average. In basketball parlance, King Kelly was a gunner. He shot a lot. The Machine Gunner, they called him. No rawboned example of Spartan living, Kelly was 6 feet 2 and weighed 215 pounds. Genes alone didn't account for his considerable size. They had help from hamburgers ("25 or 30 a week," he said), chocolate milk shakes ("one for each hamburger") and beer.

The night King Kelly scored 75 points against Maytown High, he was said to be playing under the inspiration of Milwaukee's famous export. A Maytown athlete complained to his coach that Kelly was drunk, and the coach said, "Be sure you find out what brand he's using, I'll get you some." It was Wayland's custom to carry its own drinking water in large bottles wrapped in tape. Few people believed Kelly's bottle to contain only water. "That's a myth," Coleman said of the Maytown report. "My senior year, *before* a game, never. *After* a game, well…"

Kelly was a 10th grader, he said, when he discovered it was difficult to play basketball after a bout with spirits. From his house to the Wayland gymnasium, it was a mile and a half walk. A buddy gave him a ride and asked if he'd like to share a fifth of tequila. Kelly was 14 years old. "At that time, the most I ever drank was three or four beers. I had four or five drinks of that tequila and then went to play a basketball game. My head was buzzy. That night I couldn't put one

in a truck bed. I got two goals."

During games, Coleman was not Little Lord Fauntleroy. He denied a story that he put opposing free throwers out of sorts by pulling hair on the back of their legs, just as he denied he ever scored on a fast break and continued to the concession stand for a hot dog and Coke ("I did have two or three hamburgers and a milk shake at The Fountain about 45 minutes before every game. If it bothered me, I didn't notice it.") Many of Coleman's baskets came on shots put up after running over people. One writer said Kelly had moves previously used only by Sherman tanks. "Ninty-nine per cent of the time, the defensive guy tried to jump in front of me and I was too quick for him and then he'd stick a shoulder into me. The foul was on him."

Coleman said players trying to contain him took hold of his uniform shorts. Sometimes they stood on his toes. They threw body blocks at him. "I'd see 'em coming and stop on a dime like I could. They'd fall down, and I'd step over 'em for the basket." If a defender persisted in his harassment, King Kelly might talk to him in this manner: "Hey, you're wasting your time. You're not gonna stop me. When I get the ball, you ain't even gonna *see* me." Or Kelly might embarrass the poor fellow by first holding the ball out toward him. Then, when the taunted defender lunged for the offered ball, Kelly bounced it between the guy's legs, caught it on the other side and scored. "It's a lot of fun when it works," he said.

Coleman was an outside shooter, mostly from the top of the key. He depended on an extraordinary change-of-pace move, first at full speed, then dead in his tracks, then at speed again, to free him for the instant he needed to put up

33

Kelly Coleman shooting

his jumper. The shot was not textbook perfect, in that he launched the ball from above his right shoulder instead of from the top of his head. He was a good rebounder, mostly because of his bulk and an uncanny ability to determine where the ball would bounce from the rim. "I'd just look and know where it was going," he said. "I don't know how."

On nights when it was all working — at Maytown, for instance, when he made 31 of 49 shots — Coleman played a game unknown to people less favored by nature. "I felt kinda like Cassius Clay. Floating like a butterfly. If I had to, to score, I felt like I could *jump over* anybody."

When Kelly Coleman, on March 14, 1956, walked out of the Phoenix Hotel in Lexington, leaving to play for Wayland High in the State Tournament, pieces of paper fell from the sky and people scurried after them, curious. An airplane circling the city had dropped thousands of leaflets announcing the presence in town of King Kelly Coleman, "the greatest prep basketeer in history" (to quote the leaflet). Kelly saw people picking up the papers and talking about the wonder of it all. He paid little attention, for by then the King had been the subject of so much publicity that one more piece of propaganda, no matter how ingeniously delivered, meant nothing. He was thinking only of the State Tournament. He once said he had no particular ambition in life except to win the state championship.

In March of 1956, some of the big movie stars were Alan Ladd, Joel McCrea, June Allyson, Audie Murphy, Yvonne De Carlo. Hamburger sold for 29 cents a pound and milk for 39 cents a half-gallon. In Hopkinsville, the school board voted to expel any student who got married or pregnant. The South Carolina General Assembly passed a bill ordering the firing of all public employees who were members of the National Association for the Advancement of Colored People. Integration, the legislators said, was not in the best interests of peace and tranquility. President Eisenhower said he'd "be happy to be on any political ticket" with Vice President Nixon, who'd been a source of discontent among some Republican leaders who wanted the young Californian out of office. On the radio, the Lone Ranger, Fibber McGee and Molly, Groucho Marx and Gangbusters were on the air in competition with the State Tournament. Too bad for the stars of the airwaves. For Kentuckians, it was time to tune in King Kelly.

The Coleman house on Beaver Creek was put up on seven logs in an attempt to escape the rising waters every spring. The family often moved everything from the first floor to the second until the waters receded. In March of '56, Beaver Creek was far out of its banks. The people of Wayland left home in boats to see the King play. Coleman's mother, a Baptist who had nothing to do with fun and games, never saw her famous son play basketball, save in a film. His father, Guy, moved from Wayland when the Elkhorn Coal Company, the town's creator and sustainer, closed down the mines. The elder Coleman, a strict disciplinarian who never allowed Kelly to go out at night, went to Cleveland to work in a steel mill when his son was a 10th grader. Of 11 Coleman children, Kelly was the first boy after four girls. A sister, Linda Carol, was in Lexington for the State Tournament.

Kelly hadn't always been a basketball hero. Baseball was his game. But when he tried out for the eighth-grade basketball team, he wasn't good enough to earn

WAYLAND'S
"KING KELLY" COLEMAN
Is In Town

FOUR YEAR RECORD TO DATE

Year	Games	Total	Average
1955-56	37	1734	46.8
1954-55	36	1174	32.6
1953-54	30	784	26.1
1952-53	20	386	19.3
	123	4078	33.2

Kelly Coleman Is Called Greatest Prep Basketeer In History By Adolph Rupp

By Billy Thompson (Lexington Herald-Leader)

By Billy Thompson

"The greatest high school player who ever lived . . . A combination of Cliff Hagan, Frank Ramsey and all the other great stars who have played at Kentucky."

The quotes are from Adolph Rupp, veteran University of Kentucky basketball coach.

And the player to whom he is referring is Kelly Coleman, the crackerjack cager at Wayland.

Rupp, who has been watching basketeers for lo these many years journed to Pikeville Friday night to see the heralded Wasp warrior in action.

"He is fantastic. You have to see this boy to believe what he can do —and I still am not sure I believe it.

"He can shoot any sort of a shot. Mostly, though, he fires one-handers from the head of the circle.

"He dribbbles behind his back as good as any player I have ever seen. He came down the floor in the second quarter last night, dribbled behind his back and the ball was stolen from him. A few minutes later, he did the same thing, faked his opponent out of his shoes and hit the nicest shot I have ever seen. ly and isn't too good defensively, but he sure knows what a basketball is for.

"He resembles Frank Ramsey coming down the floor. He is big (6-3 and weighs 212) and his shots don't hit the rim and roll in. They are dead center. The net swishes upward as the ball glides through.

"He can do more with a basketball than Cliff Hagan, and that is saying a lot," Rupp added.

(Both Hagan and Ramsey were All-Americas at Kentucky).

COLEMAN HAS THE AGILITY OF A 120-POUNDER

By Gordon Moore (Louisville Courier-Journal)

Kelly Coleman is the biggest discovery in the mountains of Kentucky since coal was found 0 years ago. He is not only a prolific scorer but a terrific rebounder, dribbler, and all around team-an. He never shoots when another teammate is open, and he has the uncanny knack of follow-g his own and teammates' shots for two-pointers. Once the ball is on the offensive board, he eps it in the air, never once bringing it down as most high school players do, until it goes in.

an uniform. "That really peeved me," he said, "because I could beat everybody to death in baseball." So, for the first time (and maybe the last), Kelly Coleman worked at basketball. With other Wayland boys, he played day and night on a concrete, lighted court on the town's main street. "In the ninth grade, I was All-District," he said.

"In the 10th grade, it seemed like every game I was getting better. And my junior year — people don't realize this, but it's true — I broke the state scoring record. I was getting 30, 32, 40, 42 points. I could see that the next year it'd be hard for me to get *under* 40."

The game that earned Wayland a spot in the State Tournament may have been Coleman's best ever. Wayland beat Pikeville 96-90 in the regional final at Pikeville. Although Kelly fouled out with a minute and a half left in the *third* quarter, he had 44 points. "I would've got 80 if they didn't foul me out," he said. Coleman said the game became a battle of referees, one working his whistle off for Pikeville, the other trying to keep things "honest." The box score shows, however, that six Pikeville players fouled out, and coach John Bill Trivette's team played the last 39 seconds with four men. Trivette's wife, in a comment on the officiating, socked the "honest" official, Milford (Toodles) Wells, on the head with her purse. "Toodles had a police escort out of the gym, out of town and out of the county," Coleman said.

The night of March 14, the State Tournament for the first time had a sellout crowd for the opening session. More than 13,000 people paid to see King Kelly Coleman. Many came attached by strings to helium-filled balloons bearing the single word, "COLEMAN." The

Lexington Herald carried this headline: "Kan King Kelly Kop Kommonwealth Kage Krown?"

As Wayland warmed up, eager patrons surrounded the mountaineers' end of the floor. "They were even counting the shots I missed in warmups, like I was really pushing to make 'em," he said. Though well aware of his fame — "Once in a while Kelly gave the impression that he knew his own importance, if you know what I mean," said Copper John Campbell, the Wayland coach/diplomat — Coleman yet was shocked by this lavish attention. He wasn't feeling chipper, either, because he had the flu. And the goals, standing free in the vast open space of the Coliseum instead of being tacked to the wall as they were in the mountains, seemed small. Coleman thought, "How am I going to put one in *there*?"

The worst was yet to come.

"I jumped center for us, and from the first tip, when I tipped it to a guard and he gave me the ball back, it seemed like all 13,000 people there booed me," he said nearly 20 years later.

He couldn't figure it out. "I hadn't done anything to those people. I guess I'd gotten so much publicity that people resented it. Sports writers were looking for flaws. I wasn't on the sports pages. I was on the front page, and people were against me because of it. Hell, I wasn't responsible for those papers dropping out of the sky. I hadn't hurt anybody. I was just a little kid."

The booing took a pattern. "It stopped when I didn't have the ball, and it started up again when I got it."

Kelly scored 50 points despite the distraction. "But it kinda turned me off to the people in Kentucky, even to basketball, really. Basketball lost its importance.

It wasn't fun anymore. It was a job, something I'd do just well enough to get by. I didn't even try after that. I didn't have the enthusiasm, the drive. I decided I didn't want to be a super-hero anymore."

Wayland won that first game easily, then used Kelly's 39 points to beat Earlington 65-58. That set up a game with Carr Creek, the tournament favorite. During the regular season, Wayland and Carr Creek played twice, each winning a close game. Wayland, winner in 35 of 39 games with a 91-point scoring average, figured to win the tournament if it defeated the Creekers.

As always, Carr Creek coach Morton Combs chose not to run with Wayland. To run with King Kelly was to invite him to score 50. So Coleman scored only 28 under defenses that often put three men against him (Wayland's other guard, Elmon Hall, scored 30 that night).

Wayland led 67-66 with three seconds to play.

Carr Creek's Freddie (The Ready) Maggard, whose 20-foot shot with seven seconds left in overtime won the Creekers' first tournament game, then launched a 30-footer.

"Maggard was looking for their star, Bobby Shepherd, and he couldn't find him," Coleman said. "So he shot it. It went straight through."

In the locker room, Coleman sat on the floor in a corner, weeping. A Lexington sports writer, Billy Thompson, approached and then turned away. "Don't go, Billy, you're the only guy who's stood by me," Coleman said.

Pikeville's John Bill Trivette moved toward the pair. "Those people want your blood, Kelly," the coach said of the tournament spectators.

Coleman turned to Thompson. "I'm going to give 'em the greatest basketball game they've ever seen. I'm going to get 60. And then, Billy, you tell 'em for me to drop dead."

That night Coleman scored 68 in Wayland's 122-89 victory over Bell County. "I could've got 90," he said. Excited fans hoisted Kelly to their shoulders in celebration. He only wanted down.

"I was mad. I left the floor, left the gym and went back to the hotel. I ran into a guy from Wayland in the lobby, and he gave me a brown paper sack with a fifth in it. I didn't drink it. Another guy from Wayland and I went to a little bar and I had three mugs of beer. I gave the fifth of whiskey to the other guys on the team."

Kelly Coleman said he was either in that bar or in his hotel room, reading comic books, when the All-Tournament trophies were handed out at the Coliseum. His sister, Linda, accepted for him, explaining that the King was too "shy" to come forward. Carr Creek won the tournament, pleasing romantics who remembered the ragged urchins of 1928, and Ted Sanford, commissioner of the Kentucky High School Athletic Association, said it was the greatest State Tournament ever. He never changed his mind.

As it was predictable that a drawn beer would have suds atop it, so was it certain Kelly Coleman would develop an intimate relationship with trouble. With the departure of his father for Cleveland, Kelly, then 15, was set free. His mother, Rusha, had her hands full with five younger children. Besides, at age 36 Kelly confessed, "I think I must have a little Indian blood in me. I'd get a little wild sometimes."

Myth insisted that King Kelly left several gymnasiums to the accom-

When Coleman scored 68 points in the third-place game of the 1956 State Tournament, well-wishers carried him off the floor. Coleman wasn't all that excited about it.

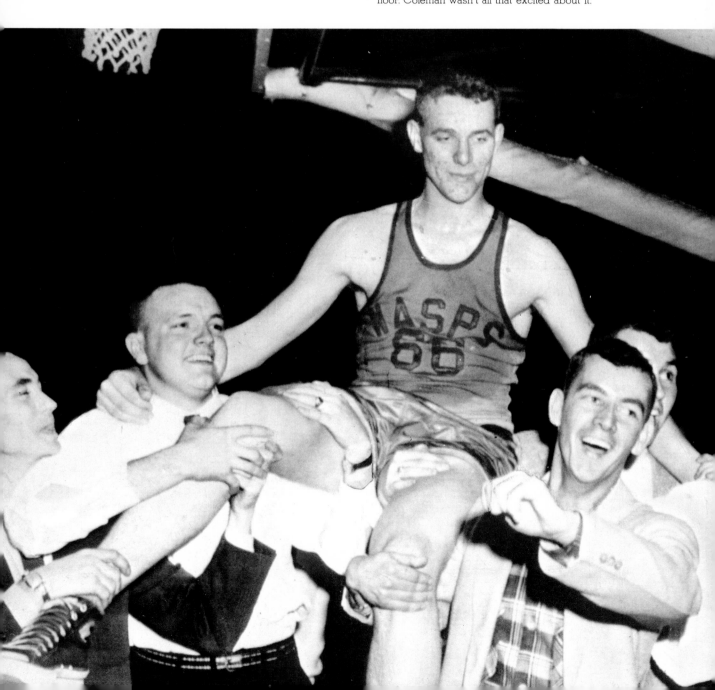

paniment of gunfire. He denied it. He also denied he was ignorant. "If you look back at my sixth- and seventh-grade records, you'll see I got good grades," he said. "That was before I became an idiot. Girls, playing basketball, screwing around — that's all I was interested in. On an IQ test, I had the highest score in the county — 142. But school was a secondary thing. That's why Little Bo Peep called my house. Lawrence B. Price, the principal. His initials were L.B.P. Little Bo Peep."

Coleman's companions were not all Sunday School teachers. Because Wayland won so often with such ease, gamblers took to betting on how many points the King would rack up. In its recruiting of him, one university sent a gambler to discuss with Kelly methods by which they could both grow rich. Pearl Combs, the old Hindman High coach, once bragged that his boys would hold Kelly to 21 points. The betting line was 35 points. "I had 39 at the half," Kelly said. "When I walked out of the gym, the gamblers all lined up and shook my hand. 'Nice game, Kelly,' they'd say. And every time I shook hands, I'd pull back a $20 bill and put it in my pocket."

At the advanced age of 17, then, Kelly Coleman had been places and done things.

It was only the beginning.

Because it recruited Kelly with feverish zeal and greenbacks awinging, West Virginia University was punished by the NCAA even before Coleman enrolled. Part of that punishment, in fact, was the Coleman could never enter the university. At the behest of coach Copper John Campbell, once an Eastern Kentucky University star and a buddy of its coach, Paul McBrayer, King Kelly signed up at Eastern — for six weeks. "And I stayed

the last two weeks just to get my monthly paycheck of $250."

University of Kentucky zealots dearly wanted Coleman. They sent a 20-foot-long petition bearing thousands of signatures certifying their desire to see the King play for the Baron Rupp. Frank Ramsey and Bob Burrow, both All-Americas at UK, whispered sweet nothings into Kelly's ear. Gov. A. B. Chandler said howdy, podnuh. Coleman said, "Kentucky offered me four scholarships — for me and three of my sisters. They'd get me and my wife a place to live. They'd see we didn't need anything. They promised I would have a business opportunity open to me when I was done playing. They offered me the world, is what they did."

How Coleman came to turn down Kentucky is a story we'll get to later.

Done with Eastern Kentucky and McBrayer — *that* is another story we'll get to later; King Kelly made things happen — Coleman worked a year in a steel mill in Middletown, Ohio, the home of his in-laws. He'd married his high school sweetheart, Ann Watkins, a majorette, shortly after graduation. From Middletown, he returned to Kentucky Wesleyan College.

"College beats manual labor," he once said.

Besides, Wesleyan did its best for the visiting royalty. "They couldn't give me the moon, but they made sure I didn't starve," he said. "They got my wife a job at General Electric. We had one kid then."

At Wesleyan he was the nation's sixth-leading scorer as a freshman (26.6 points a game). Later he walked off the court during a game, an action for which he was suspended (and which led Kelly to put the team on notice that it needed *him* a lot more than he needed it). The last game of his college career was the semifinal of the NCAA small-college tournament. He refused to play in the consolation game because he had, he said, "several other things to do that night."

He was the second draft choice of the New York Knicks, the ninth player picked in the NBA's draft that year. But he never played a regular-season game for the Knicks, and wound up in the Eastern League on a team with Bill Spivey. Convinced that the Knicks had blackballed him in the NBA — we'll get to that story, too — Coleman joined the new American Basketball League, a venture financed by Abe Saperstein, owner of the Harlem Globetrotters.

The ABL folded quickly, and, to earn his full contract, Coleman played on the United States Stars, a stooge team traveling with the Trotters.

"We had one rule on the Stars," Kelly said. "Five of us had to be sober every day. I'd be sober Monday, Tuesday, Wednesday. Then not sober on Thursday, Friday, Saturday."

Other than that, nothing much happened since Kelly Coleman left Wayland.

Now, those stories we promised . . .

✓ Why King Kelly said no to Kentucky — The Elkhorn Coal Company home offices were in Charleston, West Virginia. Word got there of the phee-nom at Wayland, and West Virginia University decided to make its move before Coleman was seduced by UK.

The summer after his junior season, Coleman was given a 1954 Dodge ("It helped my mobility with the girls"), a gasoline credit card and clothes ("All I ever had before was two pairs of pants. Suddenly, I had 15 pairs of shoes, shirts,

watches, coats — I had enough clothes to outfit our whole team"). Also, in an attempt to hide the King from UK, West Virginia gained him entrance to the exclusive, $2,000-a-year Greenbrier Military Academy at Lewisburg, West Virginia. The commencement speaker perenially was Dwight Eisenhower. Greenbrier, Kelly could do without.

"You had some 10th grader with rank pushing you around," he said. "You had to have your shoes shined. Mine never shined good enough. Lights out at 9 o'clock. No girls. They arranged blind dates, but you had to be in by 10 o'clock. For every time you screwed up, you got 10 demerits. The maximum was 250 and they kicked you out. I had the max in six weeks."

Although the academy commandant offered to wipe the slate clean, presumably in deference to the King's 20-foot jumper, Coleman went back to Wayland for his senior year — after promising he'd still attend West Virginia.

Two lawyers came to Wayland that winter, he said, urging him to attend Kentucky. Besides offering Kelly the world, they said they'd pay back West Virginia all the money it spent on him. So Kelly told them about his West Virginia dealings. "At the time, I was thinking, 'To hell with Kentucky, to hell with those people.' They booed me at the State Tournament and all I ever did was play as hard as I could, the best I could. I figured I'd been used and abused; it was time for me to use and abuse somebody."

The NCAA, snooping around on a tip from another school, uncovered West Virginia's illegal shenanigans in connection with King Kelly. "The NCAA man came to see me. He showed me the letter asking for an investigation of West

Virginia. It was signed by those two lawyers on behalf of UK. That was it. They'd used what I told them. I was still thinking about UK in the back of my mind until I found that out."

Adolph Rupp didn't remember it that way. He said King Kelly "wasn't a team player, like we wanted." Besides, the Baron said. "There wasn't any violent recruiting back then."

✓ Why Coleman left Eastern after six weeks — "McBrayer tried to operate like a Marine D.I. One time he told me to be in his office at 3 o'clock. I got out of a class at 5 'til and went straight over. I got there at 3:05, and he said, "When I say 3, I don't mean one minute past 3.'

"We ran in a cow pasture. I turned an ankle and the trainer said to stay off it for two weeks. That was a Tuesday. McBrayer made me run on Friday. I had to hobble all the way and I finished an hour behind everybody else.

"You had a spot to stand in practice. If I'm third in the front row, I better be in that spot or he'd make an ass out of me.

"If you were shooting in practice, you had your ball and your basket. If you miss a shot and somebody throws your ball back, he'd be all over you.

"He had me trying to change my shot, to get me to shoot it off the top of my head instead of the way I'd always shot. Well, hell. That nut. Six weeks was all I could take. They weren't paying me enough — $250 a month and room and board — to put up with him."

✓ Why King Kelly didn't play in the NBA — The Knicks gave him $2,000 to sign, a $1,000 bonus for reporting to camp under 210 pounds and an $8,500-a-year contract. In early scrimmages, he played well, starting at guard opposite Richie Guerin.

Coleman had decided to reform. "Maybe I'll try to play," he said describing his training-camp philosphy. "I won't drink. I won't anything."

The conversion didn't take. "Guerin one night said let's have a beer at this bowling alley. Well, we got to going. I never was one to control my drinking. And I got in a little dispute with a player who had a lot of pull with the coach, Carl Braun.

"I got no way of proving it, but I never started again, so that must have had something to do with it. Another time I was driving into town and waited 30 minutes for this big wheel. I called his room. Then I left him in bed. He got hot about it and we, shall you say, exchanged words. Then, another time, something happened in the locker room."

After a good year in the Eastern League (18-point average on the championship team), Coleman was the third-leading scorer in Abe Saperstein's ABL. The league folded then, "and guys who couldn't carry my shoes onto the floor went right into the NBA. So I called a friend of mine, Harry Gallatin, who was coaching the St. Louis Hawks. He said, 'Kelly, find yourself a good job and forget about the pros.' The NBA had me pegged not to play."

It was September of 1975. In two weeks Kelly Coleman would be 37 years old. He lived in the Ramblewoode sub-division, a new community of $35,000 homes in suburban Detroit. Then an elementary school physical education teacher, Coleman in the years since pro basketball (1) worked three years in a steel mill in Cleveland; (2) returned to

Wayland, bought a gas station and ran for the Kentucky House of Representatives ("I wasn't a politician. I thought all I had to do was get my name in the paper once a week. I didn't know I had to beat the bushes and lie a lot. I carried two precincts out of eight."); (3) sold the gas station to finance a final year of college at Pikeville College and Wesleyan, and (4) moved to Detroit, where he first taught, then worked in the promotion department of *The Detroit News* and, in 1974, returned to teaching.

"I turned down two high school coaching jobs this year," he said. "I'm too old anymore."

Coleman weighed 260 pounds. He carried the weight easily. As he moved about his living room, he was light on his feet. His eyes were a flame blue, and his brown hair was thick and wavy. He had four children: Terri, 18; Beverly, 17; Kelly, 12, and Mary Anna, 9. His son didn't play basketball. Hockey was his game.

If King Kelly had it all to do over again, would he do it differently?

"I'd cut down the partying, I guess. But back then, I just didn't care. I'd try a little more."

Regrets came occasionally. "I was the No. 1 man on the high school All-America team. Ahead of Oscar Robertson and Jerry West. Now I see them on television, making commercials. They're rich and I'm still a poor guy."

What about 1956? Almost 20 years later, did it seem, looking back, that it was real? Or a dream?

"I sometimes wonder *how* I scored so many points." Coleman laughed. "I watch games on television now, and I say, 'How could I score that many? How could I have been that cocky to think that way?'"

The King as family man. Before a game at Kentucky Wesleyan, Coleman visits his daughters, Terri (left) and Beverly, and his wife, Ann. Two rows behind the Colemans are Ed Diddle and, to his right, his assistant Ted Hornback.

The partying, Kelly? What happened when you partied?

"I guess you heard about the night I emptied the men's dorm at Wesleyan."

No.

"I thought *everybody* knew about that. It was my last year at Wesleyan. Somebody had been siphoning gas out of my car. A friend of mine had a tavern in Owensboro and he had a party for me, a farewell party because I was about to leave to go to the Knicks camp. I had me some champagne and bourbon. I got a little inebriated, I'd say.

"I got back to my apartment. Then I heard a noise outside. Someone was out there with a bucket and a hose by my car. The guy sees me looking and he runs straight into the men's dorm.

"Me, I'm about half-inebriated. As a hunter, I've got a shotgun in the closet. So I load it and go marching 250 yards across an open field to the dorm.

"I asked a couple of guys if they saw anybody run into the dorm. They said no. Now, most people were scared to death of me just being me. Being from the mountains, they figure I'm out of some

King Kelly Coleman, 1974

wild cave. Well, I cocked the hammer of that shotgun and I told 'em to go knocking on the doors and get everybody out for inspection.

"Someone called this friend of mine. They figured somebody better get ol' Kelly out of this one. My friend comes over and I tell him to go home. He says, 'Come on, Kelly.' And I say go home, and I swing the shotgun around. All I'm trying to do is find the guy who siphoned my gas. I just want to smell everybody's hands.

"I tell my friend again, 'John, if I were you, I'd head home.' He starts walking. Then, just for kicks, I fired off a round about 30 yards over his head. He did the hundred in about eight flat after that."

Did Kelly ever find the gas thief? "Nope."

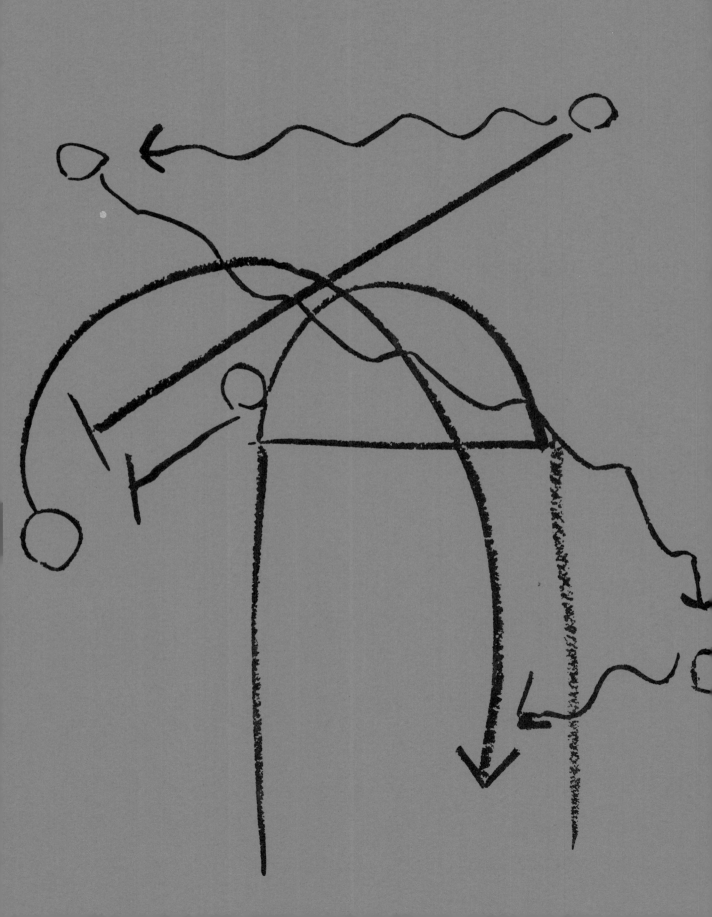

MARCH MADNESS

The Atlanta Redwings of 1959 won their first 29 games, an accomplishment that left Eldridge Carson (Doc) Kinsey Jr. near insomnia. "It gets harder to sleep every night," he told a reporter who wondered how the bow-tied coach was holding up under the pressure. Kinsey's corn town team, representing a high school with an enrollment of maybe 100, had the longest winning streak in the state. When the mighty Redwings won the regional tournament, moving within two games of a trip to the Sweet Sixteen, Atlanta's citizenry went sweetly daft. The city fire truck was commandeered for a two-block parade through the heart of town; a state legislator drew up an official proclamation of congratulations; people with convertibles rushed to give their heroes an open-air ride in the parade, and store owners painted messages on their plate glass, one of which said, "Atlanta 84, Lincoln 80 — How About That!"

Lincoln was *the* city in Atlanta's vicinity, the county seat with a population of about 17,000. Its basketball team had won the regional tournament nine years in a row. So Atlanta's victory was worth celebrating, for David had brained Goliath, and years later an anvil-footed playmaker asked Kinsey what he remembered about the great game. "You made five or six straight free throws right at the end," the coach said. Then 34 years old, old enough to know better, the playmaker yet glowed in relived glory (and didn't point out that it was, really, only four free throws).

The Redwings never expected to go to the Sweet Sixteen, nor did they ever talk about it. Such a possibility existed only in the kind of delirious imaginings that included corporeal transformation into Elvis Presley or, failing that, marriage to Elizabeth Taylor. (I can hear the playmaker proposing: "Liz, were you ever a cheerleader?") The end came quickly for the gallant Redwings, who lost to a big-city team 73-48 in the sectional tournament. There were excuses available. One regular didn't play because of a broken ankle, and two others had the flu that night. But we all knew the true explanation for the defeat. As much as a guy may dream of it, he doesn't marry Liz Taylor very often.

"You talk to Kentucky people about

McCoy Tarry was 5 feet 7. At Brewers High School, the team bench was so high the coach's feet wouldn't touch the floor. So Tarry watched games sitting on a bag of basketballs. His 1948 Brewers team won the State Tournament.

Barney Thweatt of Brewers grabs a rebound over Maysville's Buddy Shoemaker in the 1948 state championship game. Mason Cope of Brewers (22) and Buddy Gilvin of Maysville (17) are ready. Brewers was undefeated in 36 games, out-scoring its opponents by an average of 69.8 to 30.4.

basketball, and the first thing they'll say is when they went to State," said Oscar Combs, publisher of the East Kentucky Voice in Hazard. "It may be years ago, but they never forget. Making it to the State Tournament is like a man being in Louisville and getting a box seat for the Kentucky Derby — knowing it's the only time he'll ever see it."

For Warren Amburgey, who played on the Carr Creek team that won the 1956 state championship, the experience was unforgettable. "Except for my two kids being born, that's the happiest I ever was," he said. At Bohannon's Grocery in Brewers, maybe 300 miles west of Carr Creek, they remembered 1948. That's when Brewers High won it all. "We listened on the radio," Emil Mohler said. He sat by a pot-bellied stove in Bohannon's, playing checkers. "Anybody who had a radio that would pull in the game, we'd gather up everybody and go to his place."

More than 600,000 people paid over $1 million in March of 1975 to watch all phases of the girls and boys state tournaments in Kentucky. Some diagnosticians called it March Madness. The symptoms were unmistakable. One young man, stricken, took his clothes off at every game played by Lexington Tates Creek High. Not all his clothes. Mike Bowen, a senior, first pulled off a shirt. As the school band played "The Stripper," three more shirts came off, finally revealing a T-shirt with words printed on the front, "ALL THE WAY," and on the back, "TO THE STATE." For a finale, Bowen stood on the scorer's table and wriggled out of his jeans, uncovering purple polka dot shorts with "TC" painted on the rear.

Why did the young man do this act?

"It started one game when I got up and all my clothes fell off," he said.

Oh.

"It gets everybody 'up' for the game."

What's next?

"If the team goes all the way to the State Tournament, so will I." Blessedly, Tates Creek lost.

March Madness sometimes caused otherwise rational people to refer to the State Tournament as "The Greatest Show on Earth." (Sorry about that, Mr. Barnum.) The effects of the seasonal disturbance showed up in newspapers, too, where smitten scribes wrote about "The Dribble Derby." (Sorry, Mr. Pulitzer.) In looking to place responsibility for this fine hullabaloo, we might name Ralph Carlisle, John Bill Trivette, Letcher Norton, Earle Jones and S. T. Roach — five coaches who by their remarkable work, covering a period from 1928 to 1965, helped make Kentucky high school basketball the next best thing to marrying Elizabeth Taylor.

Given a glacial age to work in, a guy could write about a hundred Kentucky coaches, good ones all: Neal Arnston, Louisville Manual (whose teams won three state championships); Nolan Barger, Lexington Tates Creek; Bobby Barlow, Lexington Bryan Station; John Burr, Adair County; Bill Carter, Heath; Blanton Collier, Paris (yes, basketball); Morton Combs, Carr Creek; George Conley, Ashland; Woody Crum, Maysville/Harrison County; Julian Cunningham, Bath County; Nick Denes, Corbin; Otis Dinning, Paducah Tilghman; Ernest Fiser, Benton, and Elmer (Baldy) Gilb, Lexington Henry Clay (and longtime scout for Adolph Rupp).

Also, Delmas Gish, Central City; Robert Graves, Louisville Central; John Gross, Newport Catholic; Joe Harper, Monticello; Bill Harrell, Shelby County; Mote Hils, Covington Catholic; Homer Holland,

Sharpe; Wade Houston, Louisville Male; Jim Huter, Male; Paul Jenkins, Male (whose three state championships included two at Ashland); W. L. (Willie) Kean, Central; Bobby Keith, Clay County; Charlie Lampley, North Marshall; Bobby Laughlin, Breckinridge Training; John Lykins, Franklin County; and Lawrence McGinnis, Owensboro.

Also, Hardin McLane, Elizabethtown Catholic; Jim Morris, Louisville Flaget; Rice Mountjoy, Kavanaugh; Bob Mulcahy, Louisville Seneca; Pat Payne, Hazard; Al Prewitt, Henry Clay; Gene Rhodes, Male/ St. Xavier; Bob Schuhmann, St. Xavier; Jack Story, Cuba; Guy Strong, Male; Jock Sutherland, Lexington Lafayette; and Mc-Coy Tarry, Brewers.

Also, J. W. (Spider) Thurmond, Clay County; Barney Thweatt, Tilghman/Oldham County; Ray Vincent, Elizabethtown; Russell Williamson, Inez; Fairce Woods, Breathitt County (a quick, little man as a player, he was called "The Bantam Phantom") and Bob Wright, Ashland (whose 1961 state champions, starring Larry Conley, may have been the best ever).

Adolph Rupp called Ralph Carlisle "the best high school coach in Kentucky." Trivette was the first coach in the state to use the zone press, and he did it so effectively that even the phrase "the Pikeville press" caused opposing coaches to grow short of breath. Norton, the king of Clark County, beat the bejabbers out of a gambler in the locker room the year his team won the state championship. Jones won the State Tournament for Maysville with a bunch of midgets and finished second three times. At Lexington Dunbar, Roach, a black man, turned out great teams before blacks were allowed to play against whites. Once free of racial restrictions, Dunbar beat proud Lexington

Lafayette so many times it was said Roach ran Ralph Carlisle out of coaching and into the insurance business.

In 24 seasons, Ralph Carlisle's teams won 488 games and lost 144. He coached Lexington Lafayette to three state championships — in 1950, 1953 and 1957. The hallmarks of a Carlisle team were angry rebounding, well considered shooting, meticulous ballhandling and defense without end. "We didn't guard people with the idea of not letting them score," the coach said. "Our idea was to not give them any shots."

In that decade when Lafayette was majestic, Carlisle said his teams had three things. "First, we had a feeling of good community relations. It was an adhesive sort of thing. I'm for you and you're for me. I never had a good team without that feeling.

"Second, and this is paramount, those teams were made up of people who would accept responsibility. If I told them to learn to dribble with their left hand, they took it as their responsibility to learn to dribble with their left hand. Today no one takes any responsibility.

"Third is the innate ability of the players themselves. If they can't play, you can't win."

Carlisle was a 13-year-old kid in Lawrenceburg when the local high school basketball team played in the 1928 State Tournament. "I hardly knew a basketball from the bulb in a commode," he said. "Everybody in town said the high school had an easy game in the State that day. Against Carr Creek. From the mountains someplace. Well, Carr Creek beat Lawrenceburg 37-11. I got interested in basketball."

Later an All-State player at Kava-

48

Ralph Carlisle at work winning the 1953 State Tournament.

Carlisle and his star guard, Billy Ray Lickert, were all smiles before the 1957 Kentucky-Indiana All-Star games. Carlisle promised to "eat a door knob" if Kentucky didn't win both games. Happily for the coach's stomach, Kentucky won 91-71 and 77-76.

naugh High School in Lawrenceburg (founded and sustained by the remarkable Rhoda Kavanaugh) and an All-Southeastern Conference player for Adolph Rupp at Kentucky, Carlisle took his first coaching job in 1937 at Richmond Madison High for $1,250 a year. He was there four years and then moved to Kavanaugh for two seasons, leaving to work two years at Ft. Thomas Highlands. In 1945 he was hired by Lafayette. "It was the greatest move I ever made. They had *players!* I'd never had any players before."

By 1949 Lafayette was in the state championship game, losing to an Owensboro team that included Cliff Hagan. "Hagan was a man among boys," Carlisle said. "He could hit that hook shot better than most people could hit a crip. And if he should miss, he just went up and got it and put it back in. We won it in 1950. There wasn't any Hagan playing then."

Just as Lafayette became the standard of excellence in the state, Rupp's Kentucky teams ruled the nation. They won national championships in 1948, 1949, 1951 and 1958. The simultaneous suc- cess by coaches in the same town did nothing to make them buddies. Carlisle was openly eager to move into college coaching, and occasionally he would be mentioned as the next Kentucky coach should Rupp retire, an event forecast every spring. Carlisle said, "I'd like to succeed the man who succeeds Rupp." Since that was not a flat denial of interest, we may surmise that Rupp, an arrogant dictator who guarded his domain jealously, saw Carlisle as a threat.

"If there is any bitterness in me, it's because I was a coach with some success who wanted a college job and no one came along and said here's your opportunity," Carlisle said. "Texas A & M, Berea and Morehead offered me jobs. Nobody else. I couldn't even get an interview at Ohio State, and I could coach rings around Fred Taylor (the incumbent)."

Carlisle said Paul (Bear) Bryant, while the Kentucky football coach, once recommended him for the Alabama job. "Bryant said he told Adolph that he'd recommended me, and Adolph said, 'You did? I wish you had consulted me.' Then Bryant said, 'Ralph, I don't think that s.o.b. wants you in his league.' I said, 'Yeah, he doesn't

want anyone to make his road rougher.'"

Carlisle quit coaching in 1961 because, after 24 years and three state championships, he was being paid $5,070 — only $900 more than a first-year biology teacher. "I had a son to educate and I couldn't do that on a coach's salary. I was working six different jobs trying to get by, and it was killing me. My first year selling life insurance I made $83 less than $36,000."

Basketball was yet a part of him. "I could talk about basketball 24 hours a day for 20 days in a row without repeating myself," he said. Lean and graying, at 60 almost imperial in his manner, Carlisle sat on a sofa in his living room. His voice, always high pitched, rose a note or two with remembered excitement. There was 1957. A very good year. "Winning in '57 was probably the most outlandish deal ever," Carlisle said.

"It's like a juggler. You see him doing his act and you say that's impossible. But what you're seeing is the final product of years of hard work. The first time he tried that, he dropped things all over the place. That's how '57 was for me as a coach. All that hard work for years came together

to win a state championship.

"We had Bill Lickert, a terrific basketball player. Don Duvall was pretty fair. But the other three were not basketball players. They were smart. They could follow instructions. Eight of the 10 boys on our team were in the National Honor Society.

"In our first game, against Hartford, we beat them 16. We shot 21 free throws and made all 21. Nothing like that ever happened before in the State Tournament.

"Then we had Dixie Heights and beat them like 21. Now we had to play John Bill Trivette's team, Pikeville. They were rated No. 1 all year, and we'd been practicing all season to play them.

"We'd practiced with six men on defense every day from December on, with two guys always going after the ball. And we beat Pikeville 70-61. John Bill even called off the dogs after a while.

"Eastern had beaten Russell County in the first semifinal game that morning by 31 points. An easy one. After our game, we were held up in traffic and it took us an hour and a half to get back to our hotel. We hardly had time to get anything to eat, let alone get any rest,

51

before we had to drive back out to Freedom Hall.

"By now, I'm scared to death. We've
had no rest, and Eastern's had it easy all
day. The mental anguish of playing Pikeville, with that press, is what wore us out.
So I told my team we weren't going to
fast break against Eastern. Well, hell, that
was one of our fortes, running.

"Let me say this first. In the last
minute of every quarter, we threw the
press on — because I wanted the last shot
instead of giving it to the other team. So
in four games, we have 16 last-shot oppor-
tunities. And we scored the last points
11 times. That's because we worked on
it. It was something I'd never been smart
enough to do before.

"Anyway, now we're in the championship game and in the locker room
before the game I told my boys, 'If we
throw the ball away once, It may mean
we lose.'

"So we won 55-52 — and we *never*
lost the ball. No double dribbles, no three
seconds in the lane, no lost jump balls.
In one game we never missed a free
throw, 21 for 21, and in another game
we never lost the ball — and we won the
state championship by just three points."

Carlisle smiled. "You know, when I
was coaching, all I thought about were
the losses. Now I just remember the
victories."

"I invented it," John Bill Trivette said
of the zone press that his Pikeville High
School teams used to terrorize opponents
in the late '50s, years before such a press
became commonplace. "I'm not bragging. A lot of people say they invented it,
but *I* did."

Trivette sat on a patio outside his
home in Pikeville. He was a vigorous man,

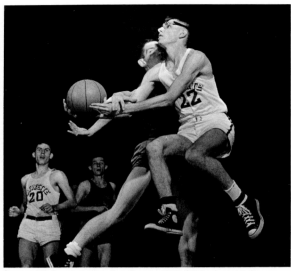

Jimmy Weiland, Lafayette, shoots. Bob Mulcahy at left.

58 years old and slight, yet possessed of
that economy of build which suggests
strength. His hair was white. His blue
eyes, unblinking, were those of a young,
aggressive battler.

"This was 1955. We played Johns
Creek. They weren't any good, and every
time we'd run a play — why, they'd be in
the way. They weren't playing by the
'rules,' by the 'book.' I became confused
and irritated because they were making
us look awful bad.

"Finally, I thought if Johns Creek
could do that without knowing what they
were doing, if it could be systematized,
it might be a real good defense.

"I sat up in bed until 3 o'clock in the
morning, considering the possibilities.
Here I was, going by the book, and the
book wasn't satisfactory. I was going to
write my own book. I couldn't wait to get
to school to see how it looked on the
blackboard. Then I told my kids, 'We're
going to do something that hasn't ever
been done before.'"

Pressing defense had been used in
Kentucky, but they were the man-to-man
variety; a defender followed his assigned
man, no one else. As late as the '40s,

defensive players were allowed no deviation from a strict man-to-man, even to the absurd point of being forced to watch helplessly as an offensive man broke free and sprinted past for an uncontested layup. The Pikeville press involved unprecedented harassment. Two and three defensive men accosted the man with the ball. "They'd get your kids rattled and then beat your brains out," said Gene Rhodes, who coached Louisville Male and St. Xavier.

Trivette saw the zone press as salvation. "When you've only got 325 kids in high school and you're playing the best teams in Kentucky, you have to have an equalizer," Trivette said. "If we played normal basketball, we'd get the tar beat out of us. We figured we'd disrupt everybody's rhythm, make them play the whole court, make them handle the ball 84 feet where they were used to handling it 35 feet, make them take three or four dribbles instead of two.

"A boy handling the ball couldn't go but three or four dribbles until he'd have to look at the ball to control it. On that dribble, the very minute his head goes down, then HIT HIM!" Trivette snapped the order and clenched a fist shut, as if grabbing an opponent by the throat, which, of course, his teams did for him. "Sometimes, the press scared a boy so much he just plain dropped the ball. We'd pick it up and get two points."

In 16 seasons at Pikeville, Trivette's teams won 442 games and lost 128. They went to the State Tournament seven times and finished third in 1957. "We were always tough and strong," Trivette said. "We didn't have big kids, but they were good-legged. All my kids played football. By playing football, they could shrug off contact in a basketball game rather than

take it as something personal."

Trivette grew up in Pikeville, where his family settled before the Civil War. He played basketball at Pikeville Academy and then the University of Kentucky for two years. In 1942, weak from an automobile accident, Trivette contracted tuberculosis and nearly died. He spent a year in a sanatorium recuperating. When the Pikeville High coach was drafted into the Army, Trivette filled in during the '44 and '45 seasons. His salary: $40 a month. After one year back at the university earning his degree, Trivette returned to the Pikeville basketball job and coached until 1960.

"I had horns this long in this region," he said, holding his hands at arm's length from his forehead.

Why?

"I was the devil. I wouldn't let anybody else win."

Trivette believed in the virtues of hard work. "We had a motto: 'Sweat in the summer and get the hardware in March.' And these kids worked. I made sure every one of my players had a goal at home. He had a ball, and I checked on him every day to see that he throwed that ball at that goal. We couldn't win on just three months' practice. I sold them on the idea it's just as easy to be a winner as a loser."

Trivette said his best team was the 1957 outfit that was rated No. 1 in the state all season. That was an unique year because a flood practically wiped out the town. So the basketball team played all its games on the road after January 25 and practiced at home only twice.

"We played Lafayette in the State Tournament. They had us 14 points at halftime. We lost by nine, and I don't know how many free pitches we missed." Pikeville had a 31-4 won-lost record that season.

Trivette, later in the coal business, wouldn't talk about why he quit coaching in 1960, other than to say, "I was mistreated." He had built a basketball team that was the pride of the mountains. In 1948 the people of Pikeville put up a 3,000-seat gymnasium for the team at a cost of $280,000. The bond referendum passed by a 10-1 margin. The gym had chair-back seats on three rows on each side, six rows at the ends.

"Do you want to see the only thing I took from Pikeville High when I left?"

Trivette said. The old coach walked down stairs inside his home, pulled on a light in the dark basement and lifted a dusty piece of canvas. Under it was an old, wooden, chair-back seat.

"My chair," Trivette said to a visitor.

"He coached in it," his wife said.

The visitor wondered why the chair had no arm rests.

"He probably knocked 'em off," Mrs. Trivette said with a laugh. "Nobody sat next to him. He'd get excited and start throwing elbows."

Trivette agreed. "I hit a little ol'

John Bill Trivette of Pikeville, 1955.

manager one night. Doubled him right up. Didn't even know I did it."

The visitor touched the coach's chair. "What are you going to do with it? Paint it?"

"No, just took it," Trivette said. "That's the only thing I took." The coach covered the chair again, turned out the light and walked upstairs.

The first six years Letcher Norton coached at Clark County High, his teams won over 30 games a year and always went to the State Tournament, winning

it in 1951. When the Clark County school administrators turned down Norton's request for a raise from his $4,650 yearly salary — "They said they ran out of money," Norton said — the coach took a job in Indiana for two seasons at $7,000 per. "But Clark County found some money when they lost 16 games in a row," Norton said, explaining how he returned home in time for the '55-56 season.

Under Norton's direction, Clark County's teams were distinguished by their compulsion to run and run and run. "The faster you could get that ball down

Pikeville's Dickie Prater (37) was a scrapper in 1949.

the floor and in the basket, the better," Norton said. He believed in a direct route to the hoop. "If some defensive player got in front of us, we didn't try to miss him. We tagged him as hard as we could. Test his fortitude, you know, to see if he'd stand in there again."

Inevitably, Clark County was scolded by purists who saw the devil's work of disorganization and chaos in fast-break basketball. Norton resented the implication that his teams played with the control of a fizzling balloon. "We ran set plays, we were not helter-skelter," he said. "On the fast break, we always had three boys in a line. They never crossed, like a lot of teams were doing then, because that just took up time. We knew what we were doing."

Norton was raised in Winchester, the home of Clark County High, and earned degrees from Kentucky Wesleyan and the University of Kentucky. His first coaching job was at Trapp High. After seven years, he enlisted in the Marines in 1941, returning to take over at Clark County in 1946. His teams' won-lost records those first six years were astounding: 30-6, 31-4, 32-4, 32-7, 34-5 and 37-2. By Norton's second season, Clark County was in the State Tournament. Norton remembered that 1948 tournament unkindly.

"We played Brewers and we had them beat," Norton said of the small-town team that would win the state championship. "We were leading by two points in the last seconds. They had a throw-in under their own basket. First time, my boy knocked the ball back out of bounds.

"The next time, the Brewers boy couldn't get the ball in and he just walked over the out-of-bounds line before he threw it to somebody. And a guy pitched

in a hook shot. The referee told me, and these are his words, 'I couldn't get to my whistle.'

"They beat us in overtime. When I went to Brewers' bench to shake hands with ol' Red (McCoy Tarry, the coach), I told him I felt that was the only time I'd really had it put to me.

"Then Brewers beat Male in the semifinals. Pap Glenn was coaching Male, and he had Brewers beat cross-ways. Brewers was better than only one team in the whole State Tournament that year. They had help to win it. Afterwards, Pap Glenn sat down and cried. A grown man. They simply took the ball game away from him."

Norton's team was runner-up in the State Tournament in '50, losing to Lexington Lafayette. It was Clark County's turn the next season when, with Linville Puckett as the star, the team won the championship. "Our biggest boy, Lewis Snowden, was 6-5 and the rest of my boys dropped down under 6 feet. But they could run and shoot," Norton said. "With those two-hand set shots, we'd tear up these zone defenses they play today. I'm talking about 35 and 40 feet out. Once we got to midcourt, we were dangerous shooters. In the 20-foot range, I stressed 60 per cent shooting."

That state championship team was the target of a gambler. Norton dealt with the unfortunate fellow personally.

"Right after the war, there was a tremendous amount of money bet on high school basketball games," Norton said. "This kid — he came from a nice family in Winchester and had been on one of my teams — contacted three of my main players. We were playing Pikeville.

"He told them he'd give them $1,000 each if they'd shave the point spread down to three points. Well, I'm standing on the court, waiting for my team to come up, and a hanger-on tells me the boys want to talk to me. That's when they told me what was going on. The guy even wanted to hold the players' watches as guarantee they'd shave the points.

"I sent my reserves to the floor, and sent somebody to get this gambler. The kid said, 'Aw, coach, I was just joking.'

"I said, 'This is not a joking business.' And my players said the guy had been after them several times. So I told him, 'I'm going to give you a good whippin'.'

"He said, 'Coach, I'm not gonna fight.'

"'Well, I am,' I said. 'So you better find some way to defend yourself.'"

Norton was a bear of a man, about 6 feet 1, well over 200 pounds. Even at age 61, he appeared formidable. Twenty-five years earlier he might have torn down buildings with his hands. "The kid had on this perky hat," Norton said. "I hit him, and he went out from under his hat. I knocked him against the far wall. My boys said, 'Coach, you're gonna kill him.' And I guess I would have.

"I jammed his hat on his head and got him by the arm — he was pretty weak-legged — and put him outside. I told him I didn't ever want to catch him in a gym where one of my teams was playing."

That was January of 1951. Nine months later, those melancholy words "point shaving" would be heard again in Kentucky. Norton quit coaching in 1962 to sell school supplies, pleasing a doctor who said basketball made the coach's blood pressure go wild. In 23 seasons, Norton won 602 games and lost 141.

Earle Jones' basketball teams won over 540 games. He's not sure of the precise number, nor does he know how many his teams lost. "We won 76 per cent of our games, I know that," he said. In 27 years, three at Kavanaugh High School and the rest at Maysville, Jones built a reputation as a perfectionist who considered fundamentals sacred. At the country club in Maysville not long ago, he introduced a visitor to Dr. Joe Knight, a chubby, balding man who sat at the bar in golfing togs.

"This man is writing a book about basketball in Kentucky," Jones said to the dentist. "I've been telling him you were the defensive star of the '38 team."

Maysville lost in the state championship game that year to Sharpe 36-27. "Long time ago," Knight said with a smile that seemed nervous.

The visitor asked the dentist what he remembered from that championship game. "Well, we lost," Knight said. "They had Jim King, the boy who went to Kentucky, and they had a boy named Culp, a red-head, who went to Murray."

Jones, the old coach, chuckled. "You remember back, don't you?"

"I remember the ones we lost," Knight said. The coach and the old player laughed together at that one. But something in the dentist's manner — the uneasy smile? — suggested the memory hurt, even 37 years later. Maybe Joe Knight once defiled a fundamental.

Jones' teams also finished second two other times: in 1930 when Kavanaugh lost a four-point lead in the last 45 seconds against Corinth; then in 1948 when Maysville lost to Brewers, the controversial conqueror of Clark County and Male in earlier tournament games. Maysville won it all in 1947, beating Brewers with a team whose tallest starter was 6 feet. "What we had then was perfect execution," Jones said. "We worked on fundamentals through hard and long practices until everything was done instinctively. You give me a thinking player, and I'll give you a fumbling player."

Fresh out of the University of Kentucky in 1928, the jug-eared guy from Richmond went to Kavanaugh when the successful Rice Mountjoy moved to Danville. In three years there, Jones coached Ralph Carlisle, Forest (Aggie) Sale and Fred (Buzz) Borries. "I'll say this, as a boastful thing, we played 'em all over

Letcher Norton of Clark County, 1950.

these 27 years. Lexington, Louisville, Ashland. We thought we could tackle them. Male, Manual, St. X, Lafayette, Hazard. That Pat Payne at Hazard was quite a coach. There was a remarkable coach at St. X named Bob Schuhmann. He was class. Blanton Collier at Paris, when he was coaching basketball, was very good. He beat me four times before I could win a game. But I wound up on top."

Sixty-eight years old in 1975, Jones had seen the development of State Tournament from 1924, when he rode from Richmond to Lexington in an open Model T Ford with curtains on the sides. He was worried about The Greatest Show on Earth.

"Teams like Sharpe, Carr Creek, Corinth — they captured the imagination of the fans," Jones said. "It looks like that day is gone, doesn't it? They started out in Alumni Gym with about 3,000 seats, and they moved it to the Armory in Louisville. We had 7,500 in there in '47. Then to Lexington, and they had 11,500 in Memorial Coliseum. Back to Louisville, in Freedom Hall, with 17,000.

"But I'm wondering what's going to happen with the State Tournament. It's getting to be a big-city affair. I'm afraid the small towns are losing interest. I know that in Maysville we had over 6,500 paid for the regional finals. The enthusiasm for the regional is like it used to be for the State Tournament."

The late, great Lexington Dunbar High School was for black students. Its basketball teams were symbols of neighborhood pride. Gymnasiums from the mountains to the Bluegrass rocked with the two customary chants of Dunbar's foot-stomping, hand-clapping, swaying-

Earle Jones of Maysville, 1947.

to-and-fro fans. "We are the Bearcats, the mighty, mighty Bearcats," the soulful patrons would sing. When the game was over, barring the rare calamity of defeat, the fans would chant, "Dunbar did it again, Dunbar did it again." Some people say Ralph Carlisle quit coaching because he heard that ditty so often.

"We lost to Lafayette in '57, the first year we were allowed to play in the Kentucky High School Athletic Association," said S. T. Roach, the Dunbar coach from 1942 to 1965, years in which his team won two state Negro championships and twice was runner-up in the integrated State Tournament. "Then we never lost to Lafayette again. We beat them 10 or 11 times in a row."

Proud Lafayette, three times the state champion under Carlisle's direction, held a 17-point lead over Dunbar in a 1961 regional tournament game. "This was to be Carlisle's last game," Roach said. "I guess that when they got us 17 down going into the third quarter, we called time out and said something. Because we went out and pulled it out 56-49.

"See, Lafayette was a very patterned

ball club. They had one play where they'd run a second guard around a screen. We'd let the first one go, knowing he wouldn't get the ball. The second man, we'd just jump out in his way every time. The poor boy, I felt sorry for him."

Did Dunbar cause Carlisle to hang up his whistle? "I've heard that said," Roach said with a quick smile. The story likely is not true, for if defeat by Dunbar were reason to go sell life insurance, the world would be overpopulated with men quoting actuary statistics. Roach's teams won 512 games (and lost 143). Too often

Dunbar's accomplishments were ignored, even as Kentucky's black teams were ignored for decades. The Supreme Court made integration the law of the land in 1954. Yet blacks were not allowed to play in the Kentucky State Tournament until 1957.

"If blacks had taken part before that, there would have been black champions years before Louisville Central won in 1969," Roach said. "Away back, Central was tremendous with Willie Kean coaching. William Falls at Hopkinsville had great teams. There was William Summers

Paul Frances of Carr Creek scores in a '48 loss to Maysville.

The spectator in the background is Ralph Beard of Male High.

at Harrodsburg, William Reed at Paris, Charles Livisay at Lexington Douglass, Vernon Coleman at Lynch, Arthur Hawkins at Mt. Sterling, James Brown at Frankfort, W. H. Goodwin at Danville Bate, Whitney Young at Paducah. They all had great black teams."

The best was almost always Central. With W. L. (Willie) Kean as coach from 1923 to 1956, Central worked wonders. They won 857 games and lost 83 (yes, 857 and 83). They won seven state Negro championships and were runners-up 10 times. They won four national Negro championships. When Central won the State Tournament in 1969, Kean's sister, Mrs. Olive Kean Boone, said it was "a dream really come true."

The night Central beat Ohio County 101-72 for the championship, the Freedom Hall crowd of more than 17,000 cheered unabashedly for the underdogs from the hinterlands (who happened to be all-white). "That was a good demonstration of White Power," said Robert Graves, the testy Central coach. "It was a shame that a Louisville team had no support except from its own people." Graves

S. T. Roach of Lexington Dunbar, 1965

said he told his team before the game to shoot for the tournament's championship game scoring record. "We hadn't scored 100 points in this tournament and I knew we could do it. I reminded the boys, too, that the people had come out to see them lose. I told them to go out and shut the fans up. We showed them."

S. T. Roach, in another time and place, worked on a similar philosophy — that the best thing an all-black team can do is simply win the basketball game. When Dunbar first played white teams in 1957, the coach told his players, "Since we are the forerunners in this thing, we can either enhance the program or kill it." His team sometimes wanted to fight on the floor, to lash out in retaliation at namecalling. "But we never did, because we didn't want to ruin the future." So Dunbar just shut them up by winning, is that it? "Our youngsters really enjoyed coming off the floor victorious," Roach said gently.

Dunbar twice played for the state championship. The first time was 1961 when it lost to an Ashland team that Roach said "compared favorably with some old Central teams, in that they were well-coached and knew what to do with the ball." In 1963, Dunbar lost to Seneca. "We could have won that tournament. We had George Wilson and James Smith, both All-Staters. They had Westley Unseld and Mike Redd. We stopped that bunch. It must have been a stupid coaching mistake that beat us."

Dunbar's basketball teams were good, the coach said, because that's what the players wanted. "Those were the days when boys gave their hearts and souls to play ball. The first seven or eight would stay at my house during a tournament. Togetherness meant a lot. They realized

Dunbar's Joe Hamilton sails in the '65 State Tournament.

James Smith of Dunbar puts one up over Seneca's Westley Unseld in the '63 state championship game. Other players are Mike Redd (24), David Hecht (23) and James Berry. Seneca won 72-66. *left*

"We are the Bearcats, the mighty, mighty Bearcats."

that if they wanted to be part of a winning club, they had to be disciplined. There was never any jealousy, any animosity on our clubs.

"Why, the girls of Dunbar were so loyal to the boys on the team that they'd say, 'All right, you spend a little time with me and then you go home to rest.'"

A visitor wondered if the coach asked the girls for that sacrifice. "I did," Roach said, eyes twinkling. "And I sold quite a few of them."

A native of Frankfort, Roach played at Danville Bate High and Kentucky State University. He coached three years at Bate before moving to Dunbar in 1941. Two years later he was the head coach there. Roach quit basketball in 1965, not long after some nocturnal gymnastics. "My wife said I'd get up in my sleep and stand on the dresser, lecturing my boys." Roach shook his head in wonder. "This coaching gets next to you."

A full house for the 1945 State Tournament in Louisville's Armory. The players, on their knees out on the floor, are talking strategy. This was before coaches were allowed to talk to their teams during timeouts.

Maytown over Clark County, 1969.

Overleaf: Not everybody wins.

Bringing home the bacon. When Earlington High won the
1967 State Tournament, Gregg and Larry Martin carried the
trophy into their house. Their mother welcomed the players,
whose father, Odell, had been bedridden since a mining
accident. They took the huge golden trophy to his bedside.
Gregg scored 20 points in Earlington's 54-53 victory over
Covington Catholic in the championship game.

Nothing beats winning an exciting game in the State Tournament. This was Caneyville over Shelby County, 1968.

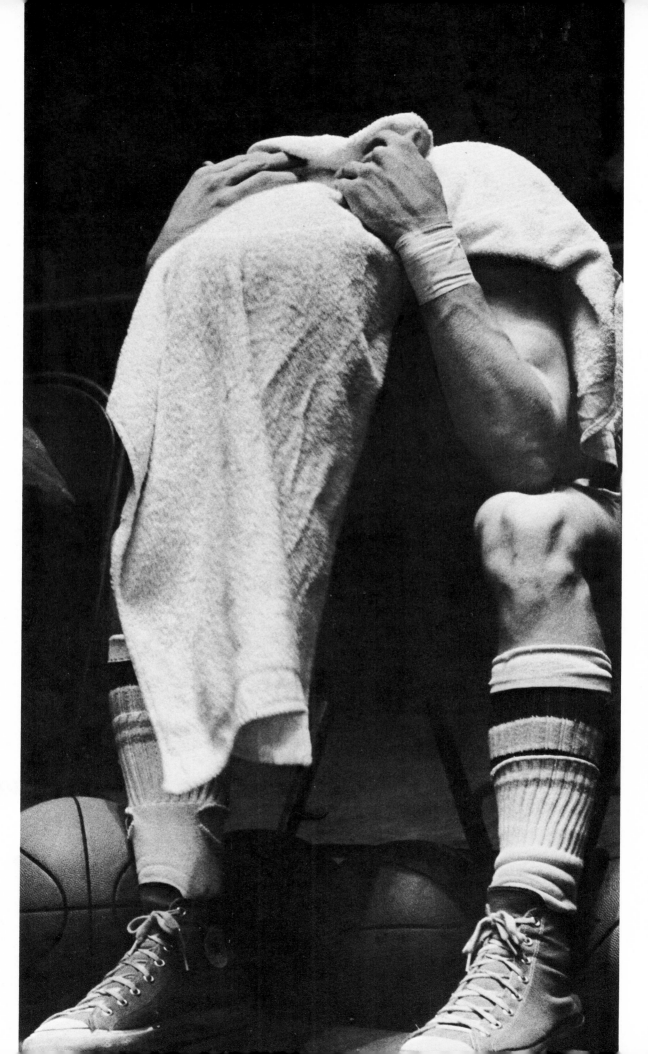

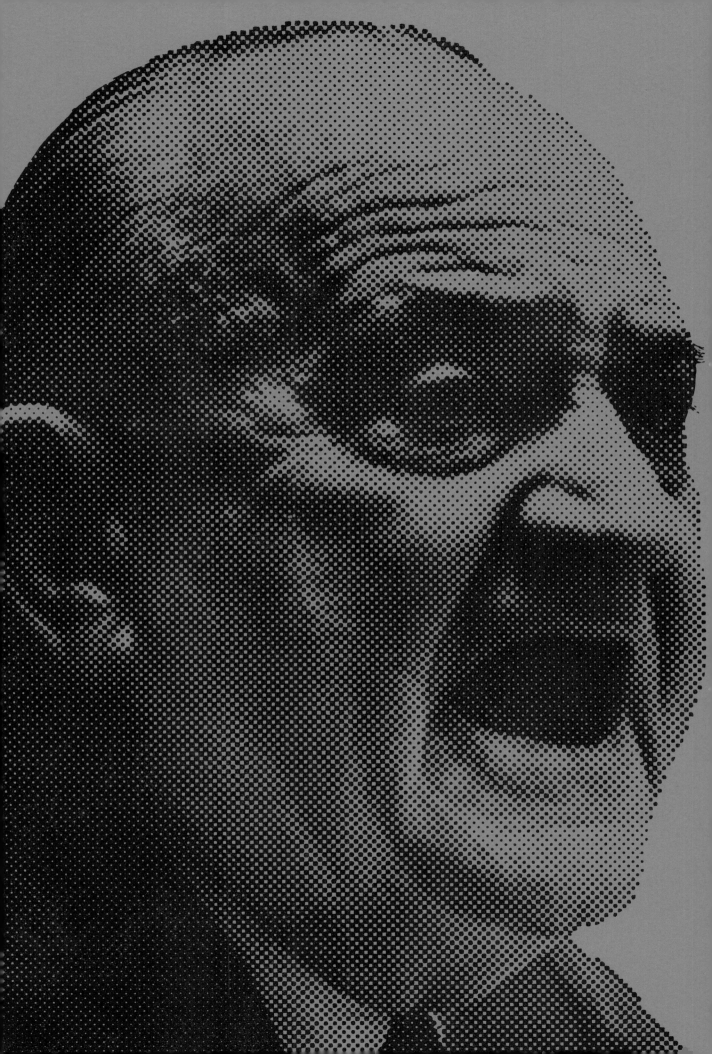

"GOOD GAWD ALMIGHTY, WHAT KIND OF PLACE IS THIS KENTUCKY?"

The man who made basketball a really big deal in Kentucky was Adolph Frederick Rupp. His teams at the University of Kentucky won a zillion games. He took the job in 1930 on the advice of a gas station attendant, and stayed until 1972, when at age 70 he was required to retire although he said he'd just as soon die on the bench, stomping his aching foot in protest of a referee's incompetence. When he was 69, Rupp said, "Retire? Why, what would I do? Time would hang heavy on my hands. It's the competitiveness I like — taking a bunch of boys and seeing what I can do with them. These young squirts come in as coaches at other places, and they say they're going to put an end to Rupp and Kentucky. Well, we'll see about that."

In his time Rupp did severe injury to modesty. Kentucky won national championships in 1948 and 1949, causing someone to ask the secret to that success. "That's easy," Rupp said. "It's good coaching." When a 29-year-old high school coach from Freeport, Illinois, made a train ride to Lexington in 1930 to be interviewed for the vacant Kentucky job, he was asked why he should be hired.

"Because I'm the best damned basketball coach in the nation," said the slender fellow whose sharp features suggested a military sternness. Adolph Rupp got the job.

And he was stern, to use a socially acceptable description of his coaching manner. "Rupp was unique," said Bill Spivey, one of two dozen All-Americas who played for him. "He wanted everybody to hate him — and he succeeded. He called us names some of us had never heard before." The resulting fear, or loathing, worked two ways. Either the player quit or he worked twice as hard. "Those that stayed wanted to show Rupp we weren't the dirty names he called us," Spivey said. Another All-America, Vernon Hatton, said, "It takes six or eight years to get over playing for coach Rupp. Once you get over it, you get to like him."

Rupp's teams from the beginning were models of simplicity and fire. They took hold of the ball and ran. That doesn't seem like much of an analysis of a system whose artful practitioners gained national fame, but then basketball is a simple game. Because Rupp won, he attracted

good players, and because he had good players, he won. It was years before any school in the South even tried to compete with Kentucky. Football was king. "Adolph winning all those games in the Southeastern Conference would be like me taking five Canadians and starting a hockey league in Texas," said an old rival, Johnny Dee. The record shows that Rupp won 80 per cent of his non-conference games, which is very good. In the SEC he won 83 per cent of the time over 38 seasons. His teams handled the ball quickly and carefully, as if it were a jewel; they rebounded at battalion strength, and they played defense in the other guy's pocket. All this the Kentuckians learned in practices run off with military precision. It was no accident Rupp and his assistants wore khaki slacks and shirts to work. Bob Cousy, the great pro, said he would pay to see Kentucky practice. And always, from the start until the end, Rupp's boys could shoot the ball into the hole. Just do it better than the other guy. Kentucky did.

Before Rupp's arrival, Kentucky teams moved deliberately. Exposure to the newcomer's radical methods bewildered the sports editor of the university newspaper, Virginia Dougherty. The week before Rupp's first game in December of 1930, Miss Dougherty wrote, "The fast break system being introduced by Coach Rupp hinges on the team's ability to move, think and act rapidly; in other words, to take their opponents by storm and drive through to a goal. The attack is a system concentrated on speed and energy. The boys of the Big Blue team have spent the past two months training and practicing in order to have inexhaustible speed and energy. However, they have been so accustomed to moving so slowly and calculatingly while using the Illinois system that when they finally get under fire the first game of the year, they are likely to be as terrified by their own speed as their opponents and revert to the type of ball playing to which they have been accustomed."

So "terrified" were Rupp's boys that they won that first game by a score of 67-19. No Kentucky team had scored more than 59 points before. By season's end, Kentucky was in the championship game of the Southern Intercollegiate Basketball Tournament, which in those days offered the ultimate prize available to teams from the Ohio River to Florida. Kentucky lost that one, 29-27 to Maryland on a last-second shot. Rupp and Kentucky would be back.

Beyond Rupp's ferocious ability to motivate players and his early realization that running was the way to win, he made basketball important not only in Kentucky but across the country by the power of his robust personality. He set records for vanity that will not soon be surpassed. The game balls at UK came stamped with Rupp's autograph. In 1970 Kentucky took a 26-1 record into the championship game of the National Collegiate Athletic Association Mideast Regional. It had been a difficult season, full of injuries, player suspensions, even Rupp's serious illness with an infected foot. Someone asked how the team did so well in adversity. "I think what held this team together was a superhuman effort on my part," the coach said. "Despite my illness, which looked like it might end my career if not end my health, I was able to pull the boys together. That did it — that and the boys' extreme loyalty to me."

The ink-stained wretches of the keyboard loved him. If a scribbler had no game to rehash, he could call Adolph, who liked to see his name in print. "Why, I'd put the center jump back and take off the backboards and net. Just leave the hoop. And raise the hoop five feet," Rupp once said to a New York writer who asked how the game could be improved. One of Rupp's players heard the outlandish suggestion and asked if the coach meant it. "Hell, no," Rupp said. "But anything for a column."

Rupp's appetites were large, whether the coach was hungry for attention or chili. "Gawdammit, what do you mean, writing that I 'wolfed' down my chili?" he said to an offending writer. Even as he spoke, Rupp wolfed down chili, the spoon disappearing into the darkness of his throat. Working on a steak, Rupp was ruthless. He said you could sort the prospects from the suspects by watching them eat. "Why, if a boy is aggressive with his eating, then he's going to be aggressive on the basketball floor," the coach said. "Lordy, you should have seen Cliff Hagan!" Rupp poked at his eight-ounce filet mignon. "See this? Hagan would have eaten this in three bites — chomp, chomp, CHOMP!"

Rupp sometimes favored a liquid diet. "I'd check the pantry to see how the bourbon was doing," he said. Bill Lickert, a UK player, once carried a suitcase for Harry Lancaster, then Rupp's assistant. Lickert dropped the bag and watched in silence as a fifth of whiskey rolled out of it. Thinking quickly, Lancaster said, "Coach Rupp always has me carry his booze." Rupp never tried to hide his pantry checking. "Some boys, at Thanksgiving or Christmas, even gave me a bottle," the coach said. "They figured it would elevate their status."

His last year at work, a tired old man,

Rupp and Joe B. Hall

The Baron watches.

Rupp sat at courtside before practice. His eyes dropped shut. "The legislature should pass a law," he said, awakening with a smile, "that at 3 o'clock every afternoon, any basketball coach who is 70 years old gets a shot of bourbon. These damned bouncing, bouncing, bouncing basketballs are putting me to sleep."

The Abominable Snowman has been spotted more often than Adolph Rupp picking up the tab. He became a wealthy man with large financial interests in cattle, land and tobacco. The magazine stand at his tidy little home on a winding street in old Lexington groaned under the weight of periodicals bringing the coach advice on how to really get rich. In his last years on the job, when diabetes and the bad foot laid him up often, the Baron of the Bluegrass cancelled all his speeches — "except for like IBM and Ford," he said. "Those people pay right well, you know." Whatever money the poor farm boy from Kansas made, he kept under a tight hold. In the melancholy days of the point-shaving scandal that would envelop UK and Rupp, the coach's grand jury testimony produced one small chuckle. He was asked who paid the check

A gentleman farmer, Rupp raised Herefords.

for a dinner party that included a known gambler. "I don't know who paid it," said Rupp. "I didn't pay it."

Rupp was often ailing, and the coach's sense of drama built each medical episode to nerve-tingling heights. In 1937, nearly paralyzed by a twisted back, he underwent corrective surgery. ("By the same doctor, Glenn Spurling, who they flew over to Europe to operate on Gen. Patton," Rupp said.) Rupp coached in a steel-and-leather corset. Later he wore an eye patch to the bench. He coached with his infected foot stretched out on a stool,

Rupp propped up his infected foot for a game in 1971.

a monarch taking his ease. He had an operation for a bleeding ulcer in 1974, and talked about it at home.

Q. What are you doing to pass the time, coach?

Rupp: "Nothing. Just sitting in my chair. Nixon says we're having an energy crisis and that we ought to conserve energy. Well, that's what I'm doing, what the President has prescribed. I'm saving my energy. I haven't moved out of the house."

Q. When did you realize you were sick?

"I was down there in Disney World, in that Contemporary Hotel. I'd just been there about three hours, and I was in my room when I got this pain in my stomach. They say childbirth is the worst pain there is. This was a hundred times that bad. I called the front desk and told them to send me a doctor.

"Pretty soon these two guys come in with a stretcher. I told them I didn't want any stretcher, I wanted a doctor. They took me away, anyway.

"Next thing I know, I'm in a hospital recovery room. A big room, big as Memorial Coliseum. There's a nurse sitting

Gingerly, the coach came home after a spinal operation in 1937.

right beside me. I said, 'Where the hell am I?'

"She said I was in the recovery room, and I said I didn't want any recovery room, I wanted a doctor. She said I'd already had a doctor. Then I conked out again."

Q. What did they do in the operation?

"They patched up my blow-out. They had to drain all these juices that had leaked out of the blow-out into my body cavity. They really put a gash in me, from top to bottom. Want to see my scar?

"While they were in there, the doctors

took out all my organs and inspected them. They said I was perfect mechanically. Then they hooked all these tubes up to me. One down my throat. That's why I'm not talking so good, this weak voice. They had things hooked up to me everywhere.

"A nurse came in every day at 6 o'clock in the morning to get blood. I told her she might as well take it from that glucose bottle, because they'd been dripping that stuff into me so much that I didn't have any blood left."

Q. Did you get a lot of calls and letters?

"That first day the New York Times called three times. The San Francisco Examiner called. The Los Angeles Times. Everybody was wanting to know what the hell was going on with Rupp. Flowers! Flowers were stacked five feet deep along the wall, and we've got letters by the sacks."

Q. Do they have you on a special diet now?

"I'm eating about what I want. I can have boiled eggs, and baked potatoes, and bananas. That kind of stuff."

Q. No chili?

"Good gawd, no. I don't know if I'll ever be able to eat that stuff again."

If occasionally cantankerous, Rupp was often capable of great charm. He said he bought a country ham and asked the store owner if he'd take a check. "I signed it in big letters, 'Adolph F. Rupp,' and said proudly to the owner, 'Do you know who *that* is?' The old guy looked at me and said, 'Well, sir, I'm a-hoping it's you.'" Asked on his 74th birthday, in September of 1975, how he'd like to be remembered, the coach talked about his 15 overseas trips for U.S. troops. He put on basketball clinics. (During one such trip, his assistant coach Harry Lancaster sent a telegram reporting that a bony 7-footer from Georgia, named Bill Spivey, was gaining weight daily. Rupp's reply was, "Damn it, Harry, I know the guy can eat — but can he play basketball?") How would he like to be remembered? "As a man who didn't shirk his responsibility," Rupp said. Tears came to his eyes. "A man who always did his best."

Rupp was inimitably theatrical in practice. He once upbraided a player who, poor fellow, hesitated briefly before shooting a layup and had the shot blocked.

"You get the ball like this" — Rupp held his hands waist high, hefting an imaginary basketball which he raised slowly overhead as he spoke again — "and then you say, 'Our Father Who art in Heaven, hallowed be Thy name, Thy kingdom come, Thy will be done, I am now going to shoot the damned basketball.'"

Rupp thought Bob McCowan, a guard, dribbled too much. "McCowan," the coach thundered. Practice stopped, as if the Great Coach in the Sky had spoken. The Coliseum was church-quiet. "McCowan, if you want to keep the ball,

Rupp's last home game was a 102-67 rout of Auburn. He thanks Stan Key, who had 23 points.

Tommy Kirby of Carmel, Ind., is pleased. So is Rupp. The coach autographs Tommy's basketball before a Freedom Hall workout.

we'll just give you a ball to take to your room and you can sleep with it. But for now, will you by damn pass the ball?"

A center, Art Laib, timidly pursued a rebound. "What's a nice Christian boy like you doing in a place like this?" Rupp said. Another center, Mark Soderberg, took a pass 20 feet from the basket. "The only time you get that far from the basket," Rupp said, "is when the roof falls in."

Rupp asked Randy Noll, "Are you writing home to your mother telling her you're not playing much basketball here at the university? Well, you're gaw-dammed right. I don't know what it is you're playing, but it ain't basketball."

Rupp asked for silence at practice. He once heard someone whistling. "Who's doing that?" No answer came. "If you want to whistle," the coach said, "we'll get you a scholarship in the music department."

The eternal verity in Rupp's personality was his love of victory. He had no patience with obvious namby-pambies who suggested, as James Naismith did, that playing well was reward in itself, that winning was not all that counted. "Why in hell do they keep score then?" Rupp said. Even the sorriest opponent put Rupp to worrying. Alabama came to Lexington for Rupp's 1,000th game. Alabama had lost 21 straight games in the conference. It lost two nights earlier by 36 points to a team Kentucky beat by 16. Someone suggested that Alabama wasn't very good.

"Now, what makes you say that?" Rupp said in his nasal twang, a scowl forming, his great fleshy ear lobes wiggling in time with his indignation. "They had Vandy down 14 points with six minutes to go, and they only lost by

"Get your hands up on defense."

eight at Baton Rouge. I'm worried, you can bet on that. My stomach feels like I've swallowed a bottle of lye. You'd think that after 40 years I'd get used to it, but I haven't."

Kentucky beat Alabama 86-71.

No one in college basketball won with greater regularity than Rupp and Kentucky his first 35 years on the job. Even before UK won its first NCAA championship in 1948 — and followed with three more in 1949, 1951, and 1958 — Rupp had been a resident four years in the Helms Athletic Foundation Hall of

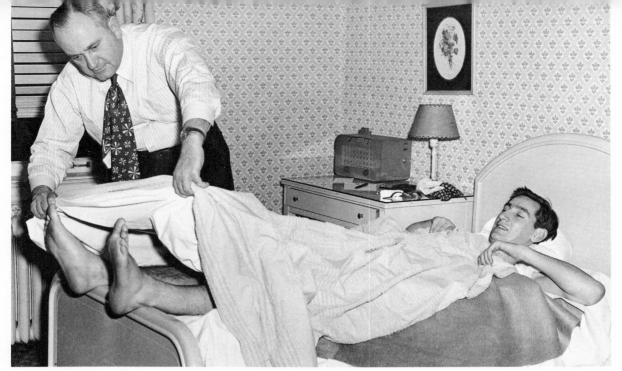
Rupp and Alex Groza ham it up on a 1948 road trip.

Fame, his place earned with an unbroken string of successes beginning in 1930.

His fame was made everlasting in those Golden Years of the late '40s and early '50s, when Kentucky ruled with power so great it was unthinkable anyone would ever match it, let alone surpass it, as UCLA and its coach John Wooden did 20 years later. Wooden, a native of Martinsville, Ind., had been an All-America basketball player at Purdue, one of the truly great guards ever. He began his coaching career in Kentucky with the Greendevils of Dayton High in 1933. They won just six of 17 games that year, Wooden's only losing season ever, while 75 miles away in Lexington the young Adolph Rupp won the first of his 27 Southeastern Conference championships. In time Wooden's UCLA teams would play Rupp's Kentuckians three times, losing each time. Wooden's last game before retirement was a victory over Kentucky in the 1975 national championship game. By then, Rupp had been in retirement three years.

Rupp never named his best team. So we are left to our own assumptions. We might well pick the 1949 team, for in a review of his career Rupp said one of his most painful disappointments was failure, in 1949, to win both the NCAA and the National Invitation Tournament (NIT). In those days the tournaments were tooth-and-nail rivals for national prestige. Ordinarily the acceptance of an invitation to play in one automatically put a team out of consideration by the other. To be invited by both, then, was proof certain that a team was so good the tournaments would lose face without its presence. No team had won both the NCAA and NIT in the same year. When Kentucky accepted invitations to both in 1949, sports writers spoke of an unprecedented sweep of the NIT and NCAA as the "Grand Slam."

"We wanted the Grand Slam, and we had the team to do it," Rupp said.

Nearly half a century before Adolph Rupp dreamed of a Grand Slam, his father died. Rupp was 9 years old, one of five boys and a girl left with their mother, Anna, to run a 160-acre farm on the plains of southeastern Kansas. His parents, German immigrants, settled there on a homestead grant signed by President

Ulysses S. Grant. Three straight crop failures preceded the death of the elder Rupp. Young Dolph, as the family called him, made money by pitching neighbors' wheat and working the shelves at Williams' Grocery in Halstead, a little town seven miles from the Rupp farm. For entertainment, Dolph swam and fished in Little Emma creek and played basketball, either in the dirt at the District 33 one-room school in Harvey County or at home, where the boys rigged up a barrel-stave hoop and threw a gunny sack full of grain at it. "That ball never bounced

too good," Rupp said.

Rupp was independent, ambitious and strong-minded, as his mother needed to be to hold the family together. When the Halstead High School basketball coach went off to World War I, Rupp took over the team himself. A substitute, Eugene Thornhill, remembered Rupp wanted to be the team captain. "He came to me and said, 'I'll see that you play that first game if you vote for me,'" Thornhill said. Dolph was elected, and Thornhill played.

In 1919 Rupp went off to Kansas

Rupp raises his arms when the striped-shirted so-and-so's hurt him.

University in Lawrence, 150 miles from home. As it happened, two other men arrived at KU that year, one an old man with a walrus mustache who had left his job as the university's manager of athletics to work with the YMCA overseas during the war. James Naismith. The other man was Forrest (Phog) Allen, young and fiery, who had been hired to coach basketball. Naismith had created the game; Allen would show it could be coached despite the inventor's original advice that you simply "throw the ball in and let 'em fight over it"; and Rupp, 50 years later, would join both of them in the Naismith Memorial Hall of Fame.

Six feet one and slender, Rupp was a center at Halstead, where the team won 17 of 20 games his senior year. Games were played in the Halstead city hall. The ceiling was only 3½ feet above the baskets. Wire waste baskets nailed to the ceiling protected eight 300-watt light bulbs. It was no stately pleasure dome, but it put other places in the shade: At Sedgwick, they played in a general store with a burning stove in one corner; at Burrton, the court was in a garage and cars were pushed out to make room for basketball; at Moundridge, the sound of leather thumping against wood filled an old church.

Kansas University, under Phog Allen, was the Big Time shortly after the war. In Rupp's senior year, 1923, KU won the Missouri Valley Conference championship, losing only one game all season. Claim was made that Kansas was the best in the nation. Two KU players were All-Americas, and another would make All-America the next season. None of them was named Dolph Rupp. No matter. If Rupp never played much — he wasn't big enough to be a college center,

nor was his ball-handling good enough to let him play guard — the intimate contact with Allen's unabashed ambition was worth some bench warming. A day would come when the firebrands Allen and Rupp would coach against each other, Kansas against Kentucky. Rupp would win.

In the spring of 1930, when Adolph Rupp's Freeport team had finished a 20-victory season, Johnny Mauer, the coach at the University of Kentucky, quit his job in a huff. Three years earlier he came to Lexington from the University of Illinois, hailed as the "Moses of Southern basketball." With him Mauer brought the deliberate style of play he learned as captain of the Illinois team. Because Mauer taught his players to crouch low when bouncing passes, his teams were said to mount a "submarine" attack. It was his job, when hired in 1927, to breathe new life into a Kentucky basketball program that once showed signs of promise.

They first played basketball at UK in 1902, a year after the game caught on at Transylvania University and Centre College. No one paid attention — to the UK boys. The girls team sent the 1904 yearbook authors into rhapsodies: "Successful from the start — two years ago — basket ball as played by girls caught not only the student, but the public favor as well, and every game played drew enthusiastic houses which packed the standing room to the door — an appreciative crowd of fellows — mad, riotously mad, over contests abounding in snappy, spectacular plays." The UK girls played two games, winning over Georgetown College 14-10 and pole-axing Jessamine Female Institute 28-1. The boys rated no yearbook report, save

84

History here. Dr. James Naismith, who invented basketball, is the mustachioed gentleman in the middle of the 1923 Kansas University team portrait. To the doctor's right is the Kansas coach, Forrest (Phog) Allen. The sturdy youth at the left end of the back row is Adolph Frederick Rupp.

Johnny Mauer, Rupp's predecessor at UK.

to note they had a 1-3 won-lost record.

By 1908 UK charged admission to boys games, lifting 25 cents from each customer, but it wasn't until 1912 that the basketball team knew success. It was undefeated in nine games. Two years later, UK's two defeats away from home were attributed by the yearbook to "much bumping over the C. & O. right-of-way," and the 11 victories positively wowed the students. "In spite of its distance from the pool room, Patt Hall and other central points, the Auditorium games drew like porous plaster, and big crowds saw every game."

National recognition came to the state of Kentucky in the 1918-1919 season — to Centre College, not UK. With a team that included John Sherman Cooper, Ed Diddle, Bo McMillin, Red Roberts and Madison Bell, Centre was undefeated in 11 games under the coaching of Professor Theodore Gronert.

UK's moment came March 1, 1921, in Atlanta, Ga., when a skinny, flop-eared boy named William S. King stepped to the free throw line. Regulation time had expired with the score tied in the championship game of the first Southern Intercollegiate Basketball Tournament.

Fuzzy Woodruff, a sports writer from Atlanta, squeezed the moment of King's free throw for all its drama. He wrote, "This decides the game," a thousand whispers say. The great building is suddenly stilled. No one talks. No one even breathes. No one dares to think.

"Bang! It's the timer's signal that the twenty minutes of playing time has expired. The rules permit the attempt at goal, however. King takes a new stance. The crowd takes another breath, a deep one. King is coolness personified. He hasn't been particularly good on foul goals all night, and Georgia has hopes, though it fears the worst. The ball leaves his hands and King's eyes do not even follow it to the basket. It strikes a rim and then slowly falls over to the right through the network. In a second he is in the arms of his comrades and is being hoisted to their shoulders."

The UK yearbook said King's free throw, which beat Georgia 20-19, lifted Kentucky to "the climax of her basketball history. The Wildcats had won the championship of their South — the first official championship of the South. The student body became an aggregation of hero worshipers, and the Blue and White quintet became the acme of things basketball."

Coaches then were little more than chaperones, keeping occupied until fall when they would begin their real jobs as assistant football coaches. When UK fired its football coach, Fred J. Murphy, in 1926, it replaced him with Harry Gamage, who came from Illinois and brought assistant coaches Bernie Shively, later the UK athletic director, and Johnny Mauer, who let everyone know that he preferred basketball. Mauer's three basketball teams at UK were distinguished by two facts: They won a lot of games (40 of 54) but never did much good in the Southern tournament.

In '29, UK won nine of 10 games in the Southern Conference, but lost in the semifinals of the post-season tournament, marking the third straight time Mauer's team failed to reach the championship game. The school newspaper said, "The Wildcat team plays orthodox basketball, and previous tournaments have proven the fact that an unconscious flip and run game fits best in the excitement and strain of a long tournament."

Mauer resigned not long after that. He was upset because UK offered him only a $300 raise for two years while giving the football coach, Gamage, a bigger raise for five years. And Gamage's team had won just 13 of 26 games. Mauer left to coach at Miami of Ohio and later at Tennessee, where he sent teams against Kentucky and Adolph Rupp (at Tennessee from 1938 to '47, Mauer won nearly 76 per cent of his games — but was 7-14 against Rupp.)

Rupp was one of 70 applicants for Mauer's job in the spring of 1930. From Kansas University, he went to Burr Oak, Kansas ("I got out of there in a hurry") and then to Marshalltown, Iowa, on the mistaken notion he would coach basketball. Instead, he was the wrestling coach. After two years there (he was the head basketball coach the second season), Rupp went to Freeport, Illinois, where in four years his high school basketball teams won 67 games and lost 16. Freeport finished third in the State Tournament in 1928 and had a 20-4 record in 1929.

Though the state of Kentucky had known wide success in both college and high school basketball — Rupp saw Ashland and Carr Creek play in the '28 national tournament in Chicago — Rupp wasn't certain Lexington was the place for him.

"Bear in mind that where Memorial Coliseum now stands, there were 55 little Negro one- and two-room shacks back then," Rupp said years later. "Bear in mind that I got a cab from the Southern Depot to Alumni Gym, and we went through an awful area of town.

"They took me to eat at the university cafeteria and out the third-floor window I

Heroes of 1921: Basil Hayden at left, with William S. King.

could see all those little Negro shacks. I wasn't used to anything like that.

"Then I had four hours to kill. I took a cab to the YMCA. In Freeport I lived at the YMCA, and I had a fine, nice room in a modern, brand-new YMCA. Well, I had a room at the Lexington YMCA that wasn't fit for a cat. I said, 'Good gawd almighty, what kind of place is this Kentucky?'"

Back home in Freeport, Rupp decided to take the Kentucky job against the advice of his high school principal, who correctly pointed out that Freeport's gymnasium was better than the university's and that Rupp's high school salary of $2,800 was the same as that offered by Kentucky. Rupp made up his mind during a walk in downtown Freeport.

"I came to the Conoco gas station. Red Greb, the owner, was up on a ladder adjusting a sign. He was a basketball fan, and he asked what I was doing downtown. I told him I couldn't decide what to do about Kentucky. He said, 'Adolph, you'll be a damn fool if you don't go. You can always go to a better job from Kentucky. It's rare for a high school coach to get a university job.' So I did it."

Forty-five years later at home with his feet up on a footstool, Rupp said he had had one misgiving on arrival in Lexington. "The thing that bothered me was how much smarter these other college coaches would be than me just coming out of high school."

Were they smarter?

"Not smarter. But they had this experience. I just wondered if the style of play I brought — the fast break — could cope with theirs." Rupp smiled. "It worked out nicely."

When did Rupp's team first hit it big nationally?

"Our first break came with Notre Dame. We had to go up there. They beat us six straight times before we got good enough to beat them." Rupp picked up a UK record book from a table near his easy chair. "Later we beat Notre Dame possibly nine times in a row." (It was nine.)

"Playing teams like Notre Dame, that's what made us as competitive as we were in our league. I can't see why anybody would play set-ups. Well, they say Adolph played Berea and Georgetown. They were on the schedules I inherited.

In those days, remember, you couldn't go to Virginia. It was too far away. North Carolina, by gawd, you couldn't get there. Twenty-four hours on the train. Through Knoxville."

Rupp's first team in 1931 was 15-3. Was he happy with that?

"I had to be. Everybody here was pleased. Let's look it up." Rupp thumbed through the record book. "Yes, sir, we won our first 10 games in a row before losing at Georgia and Clemson. Then we won the rest of the way until the finals of the Southern Conference tournament in Atlanta.

"I'll always think that game should've been an overtime. They let the clock run on us. Bozo Berger of Maryland got the center tip and let one fly from the middle of the floor right at the end of the game. It went in and they beat us 29-27.

"We got here in Lexington about 7:30 or 8 by train that night. There were several thousand people at the old Southern Depot to meet us, and we walked from there to Alumni Gym for a big celebration and everybody wound up dancing. Then I went home, took a shower and went to bed. That's how we celebrated in those days. Take a shower and go to bed."

What was Rupp's first great team?

"Oh, there's no way to tell about it. That first year was pretty good. The next year we were 15-2 and then we were 20-3. That was Aggie Sale's senior year. We won the tournament that year. They hadn't done that since 1921. That was possibly the first good team we had.

"That next year, 1934, we were 15-1 and Florida beat us in the first game of the tournament. Look at these scores — 55-16 . . . 44-12 . . . 60-15 — hell, we had some good scores in those days."

Like Mauer, Rupp was an assistant football coach at UK — handling the ends and freshmen — in addition to his basketball duties. "After four or five years, I quit fooling around with football," Rupp said. "And that's when we started dominating basketball in the South."

By 1944 when Rupp was admitted to the Helms Athletic Foundation Hall of Fame, he had coached seven All-America players: Forest (Aggie) Sale, 1932-33; Ellis Johnson, 1933; John (Frenchy) De-Moisey, 1934; LeRoy Edwards, 1935; Bernard Opper, 1939; Lee Huber, 1940-41, and Bob Brannum, 1944. (The list eventually reached 25 players with the additions of Jack Parkinson, 1946; Ralph Beard, 1947-48-49; Alex Groza, 1947-48-49; Wallace (Wah-Wah) Jones, 1949; Bill Spivey, 1951; Cliff Hagan, 1952-54; Frank Ramsey, 1952-54; Bob Burrow, 1956; Vernon Hatton, 1958; Johnny Cox, 1959; Cotton Nash, 1962-63-64; Pat Riley, 1966; Louie Dampier, 1966, and Dan Issel, 1969-70.)

In time Kentucky's playmates in the South grew tired of the bully from Lexington and decided to fight back. Schools once content to hand over basketball to an offensive line coach, with games to be played in quonset huts, hired real basketball men and built arenas so glittering and so large that UK's Memorial Coliseum, an 11,500-seat wonder upon completion in 1950, became just another pretty place. The turn of events came full cycle in 1974 with plans in Lexington to build a 22,000-seat Rupp Arena. That pleased the old coach, who mentioned another Lexingtonian when he said, "I can't think of anything named for Henry Clay."

As dominant as Rupp's teams were in the South in his first decade and a half

at Lexington, Kentucky's first truly national recognition came in 1946. A freshman named Ralph Beard was the hero when Kentucky won that year's National Invitation Tournament in Madison Square Garden. By then UK had won the Southeastern Conference championship eight times in the league's first 13 years — and would win it the next seven years in a row. Rupp's teams won the SEC 27 times in 39 seasons. Of all the curmudgeon's creations, the one touched with immortality was the "Fabulous Five." The players were Beard, Alex Groza, Kenny Rollins, Wah-Wah Jones and Cliff Barker.

They won the first of UK's four NCAA championships in 1948. The next year, Dale Barnstable replaced the graduated Rollins and UK won the NCAA again.

Kentucky became the only three-time winner of the NCAA in 1951 with a team led by Bill Spivey, a 7-footer from Georgia, and two homegrown youngsters, Frank Ramsey of Madisonville and Cliff Hagan of Owensboro. Ramsey, Hagan and Lou Tsioropolous led UK to an undefeated season in 1954 (but the team declined an NCAA invitation because the stars were graduate students and so ineligible for post-season play).

UK won its fourth NCAA in 1958 with the "Fiddlin' Five," which earned its nickname by "fiddling around," as Rupp said, and yet winning. The stars were Vernon Hatton, Johnny Cox and Odie Smith. In '66, "Rupp's Runts," with a big man 6 feet 5, took the old coach within one victory of a fifth championship, only to lose to Texas Western. (Rupp first blamed the defeat on his guards' sloppy ballhandling; then he said it was the flu that felled a starter; then he decided Texas Western was an aggregation of crooks illegally recruited, a charge refuted by the

Rupp's first team. It was 15-3 in 1930-31. Front row: Ercel Little, George Yates, Carey Spicer, Forest (Aggie) Sale and M. J. Cavana. Second row: George Skinner, Allan (Doc) Lavin, William Trott, Jake Bronston, Louis McGinnis and Cecil Bell. Back row: Rupp, William Congleton, William Kleiser, Ellis Johnson, Charles Worthington, Darrell Darby and manager Morris Levin.

In 1941 Kentucky played its home games in Alumni Gym. Marvin (Big Train) Akers steams in for a layup against arch rival Tennessee. Kentucky won 37-28.

UK's first national champions, the 1946 NIT winners.

NCAA; even later, the flu became an epidemic by Rupp proclamation, with four players ailing. The coach never lost gracefully.)

The 1970 team, starring Dan Issel and Mike Pratt — and held together by the coach's self-proclaimed "superhuman effort" — was Rupp's last with the look of greatness. It lost in the Mideast Regional championship game. Not that it mattered much, because by then everyone was playing for second place. UCLA, with Wooden coaching marvelous players, was invincible.

In 1949, the year Rupp boldly sought the "Grand Slam," it was Kentucky who walked unafraid. Beard, Groza, Jones and Barker were seniors, all back from the "Fabulous Five."

Going into the NIT against Loyola of Chicago, Kentucky had won 29 games and lost but once. Loyola figured to be easy pickings, and the bookmakers made UK a 10-point favorite. The point spread was duly reported in both the New York and Louisville newspapers, for in the years immediately after World War II the country was caught up in a giddy sports

Kentucky's first NCAA championship came in 1948.

and gambling spree, all fun and games after so much terror. Just three years earlier, players from Brooklyn College admitted taking $3,000 from gamblers to "shave" points; they were not paid to lose games, but only to make certain they did not exceed the bookies' point spread. If the bookies made Brooklyn a 10-point favorite, say, the involved players were committed to seeing that their team did not win by more than those 10 points. A bad pass here, a traveling violation there; whatever it took to win by fewer than 10 points. Naturally it was possible, in these circumstances, to lose a game — either by design, by troubled conscience or, perhaps, by simply being outplayed on that night. A *Courier-Journal* news story in 1949 carried the headline: "Bookies Give Up Net Play." Reporter Pete Johnson wrote that local bookmakers had been stung by so many upsets they were no longer taking bets on basketball. The latest upset had been St. Xavier's victory over Valley. A high school game.

When mighty Kentucky, a 10-point favorite, lost to Loyola 67-56 in the 1949 NIT, Rupp faced reporters in Madison

Square Garden and said, "We were flat, awfully flat...That's all there was to it." The Kentucky locker room was silent, save for the splashing of water from showers.

Someone asked the coach why his team was flat.

"Well, sir, I can't figure that out..."

Rupp would say, 25 years later, that he drank a fifth of whiskey in his hotel room that night, trying to figure out what happened. Bernie Shively, the UK athletic director, was with him. "Something's wrong with this team, Shive," Rupp remembered saying.

NCAA champs a third time in 1951. Front row, from left, Lou Tsioropoulos, student manager, C. M. Newton, Bob Watson, Cliff Hagan, Skippy Whitaker, Frank Ramsey; rear, trainer Smokey Harper, Dwight Price, Bill Spivey, Guy Strong, Assistant Coach Harry Lancaster, Coach Adolph Rupp, Roger Layne, and Shelby Linville.

When this Seattle player finally gets hold of the ball, he may wish he hadn't. UK has him surrounded with Johnny Cox (24), John Crigler (32) and Don Mills (54). UK beat Seattle 84-72 to win the 1958 NCAA championship in Freedom Hall.

With this layup Cliff Hagan of UK set a SEC tournament scoring record in 1952. He had 110 points in four games. Under the basket is Bob Pettit of LSU.

With the NCAA yet to be played, Rupp wasted no time in mourning. "I worked their asses off," he said. "Illinois rode on the same plane with us. They played cards all the way to New York. I wouldn't let our boys play anything. I told them to get their minds on the game. We'd already thrown one away, now let's get this one."

They did it easily, beating Villanova 85-72, Illinois 76-47 and Oklahoma A & M 46-36. In the locker room after the championship game, Rupp did a celebratory jig, at one point draping an arm around the broad shoulders of Alex Groza and doing a high kick. "Look Alex," said Ralph Beard, "Adolph's dancing!" More fun was in store in March of 1951, when Rupp and UK won a third national championship. And on August 15, 1951, shortly after new disclosures that some college basketball players had taken bribes to shave points, Rupp reacted pompously. "The gamblers," he said, "couldn't get at our boys with a 10-foot pole."

Dan Issel (44) and Mike Pratt led Rupp's last great team in 1970.

Rupp's Runts. From left are Pat Riley, Larry Conley, Thad Jaracz, Tommy Kron and Louie Dampier.

Rupp dances with Alex Groza after winning the '49 NCAA.

"YOU CAN'T DIE"

If Kentucky ever had a player in whom the fires of competitive zeal burned with a greater roar than in Ralph Beard, his name is a secret. A nation of newspaper readers often comes to know its sports heroes by the repeated use of photographs capturing the man at his moment: Babe Ruth swinging a 48-ounce bat, looking skyward; Arnold Palmer with that mile-wide smile in celebration of a successful putt. For Kentuckians who adored Ralph Beard, he forever will be the little guy, stern-visaged and hard-muscled, flying...always flying...for another layup at the end of a sudden sprint that left the enemy wondering where he went. Clair Bee, one of basketball's best coaches, said "Ralph Beard is what this game is all about." Early in Beard's sophomore year, Adolph Rupp said, "He's the greatest basketball player I ever saw." Beard was three times an All-America, twice the college Player of the Year.

In his second year as a pro, Beard was All-NBA with Alex Groza, George Mikan, Ed Macauley and Bob Davies. Beard scored on that lightning layup with either hand, shot well from outside and played defense as if points scored on him were personal insults (they were; alseep in bed, Beard once squeezed a pillow to his chest, muttering, "I've got you, Jerrell, you son of a bitch.") The well-spring of Beard's talent was an extra-ordinary single-mindedness. "To me, basketball was *everything*," he said. "Some people have brains, some people are good-looking. I was quick and I could play basketball. I had the God-given ability to play basketball and I used it."

Beard's four years at Kentucky were days of glory. As the Yankees dominated baseball, lords of all they surveyed by virtue of trainloads of supermen, so did Kentucky bestride college basketball. If Beard were special, he was only one of several. Two All-Americas could not make UK's starting team and when one pouted, Adolph Rupp publicly announced the fellow's telephone number in case anyone wanted Kentucky's discards. These four years, Kentucky won 128 games and lost nine; it won the National Invitation Tournament when that event was the nation's best; it won the NCAA twice and it helped the United States win the Olympics.

For Beard, it was Hero Time. Somebody paid $25 to a March of Dimes benefit program for the privilege of hearing Ralph sing "Rock-a-bye-Baby." If Beard needed a new suit to start school in the fall, he'd get it from a fan in Lexington. When Beard and Kentucky went to New York, a former UK football player named Nick Englisis came to Beard's hotel room. Englisis then was a chauffeur in Brooklyn, but Beard remembered him. "They called him The Greek. A little fat guy, with glasses like the bottom of Coke bottles. He was always saying, 'Ah, The Greek is schmarrt.'" Englisis first gave Beard $20. "I figured he'd won a hundred betting," Beard said. Fans and friends gave Beard $5, $10, maybe $20. "No new car, not $200 a month," he said later. "Necessities, not luxuries." They even gave Ralph Beard his chewing gum. A newspaperman in 1948 asked Beard about his addiction to the stuff.

"How big a wad of gum do I chew during a game? Oh, I'd say a hunk of five cakes...Yes, sir, I chew even when I ain't playing...That is, except when I'm asleep or eating...The year around? Oh,

Ralph Beard flying.

yes, sir, the year around...No, sir, I don't prefer any particular brand...You say that costs me about $36.50 a year?...Oh, no, sir! A drug store in Lexington gives me all my gum for nothing. They give it to me in cartons."

Upon arrival in London for the 1948 Olympics, Beard asked a store clerk for three packs of gum. "Gum!" the clerk said. "We haven't seen any gum since the Yankees left."

Beard stopped. "You mean they don't sell gum in England?"

"That is correct."

"Somebody's crazy."

In the U.S., a gum company recognized a hero in distress. It sent Ralph Beard a dozen cartons.

With 40 seconds to play in the championship game of the 1946 NIT, Kentucky and Rhode Island were tied at 45-all. Beard, a freshman barely 18 years old, was to shoot a free throw. Rooting for the underdog Rhode Islanders, most of the 18,475 spectators in Madison Square Garden set up a din intended to disturb the rookie who could win a national championship for Kentucky, its first ever.

Beard put a few good chomps on a wad of gum "that would bluff even the biggest and most contented cow on the continent," a sports writer said. "I just wanted the ball so I could shoot," Beard said. "I was scared to death."

The precocious youngster made the free throw and UK won 46-45. It was a suitable end to a tournament in which Beard scored 38 points and allowed his opposite numbers only 12. Senior All-Americas have had seasons without the success Beard realized in his first year, but for Beard it wasn't enough. He pestered Rupp for work, asking the coach to write a letter telling of his weaknesses.

The hero. As an 18-year-old freshman, Beard won the 1946 NIT for Kentucky with a free throw in the last minute. His mother, Sue, met him at the airport the next day.

Rupp advised him to improve his free throw shooting, use his left hand more and develop a 15-foot jump shot. "If you can correct these few weaknesses," Rupp wrote in the summer of '46, "you will not only be a greater basketball player, but you will be almost a perfect basketball player."

Beard took the Baron's word as gospel. "Some guys say they hated Rupp. Not me. He was it as far as I was concerned. If he told me to run through a brick wall, I'd have backed up as far as it would take," Beard said. "I wanted to show him I was the best basketball player who ever came down the pike."

In Beard's sophomore year, UK again reached the championship game of the NIT. But this time, Beard didn't score a field goal and UK lost to Utah 49-45. It was a defeat that Beard later would couple with the mystifying loss to Loyola as just one of those things, "like Jack Fleck beating Ben Hogan in the U.S. Open."

Until they let the air out of the last basketball, the Kentucky season of 1947-48 will be the measure of greatness in the Bluegrass, for in Beard's junior year his team won not only the national championship but, in partnership with the Phillips Oilers, also won the Olympics in London. "My greatest thrill," Rupp said, "had to be that Olympic team when the kids stood up there in Wembley Stadium and got their gold medals."

That team was the "Fabulous Five." Groza, 6 feet 7 and wonderfully agile, was the center. Wallace Jones, known as Wah-Wah because a baby sister couldn't handle the proper name, was a powerful 6-4 forward who could shoot from outside. The other forward, 6-1 Cliff Barker, kept the ball moving, either on the fast break or in UK's pattern offense (he often used behind-the-back passes and in time developed a bounce pass with so much spin it would come to the receiver at a 45-degree angle).

With Beard at guard was Kenny Rollins, a 6-footer with good speed. "That was the year we were best," Beard said. "And Kenny Rollins was the reason. He was the catalyst, the unselfish one." The only senior on the starting team, Rollins had been elected captain the year before. In the semifinal game of the 1948 NCAA Tournament, UK played defending champion Holy Cross whose star, Bob Cousy, had inspired a banner-maker to hang a bed sheet in Madison Square Garden: COUSY — THE GREATEST. Going against Rollins, Cousy scored only one point. UK won 60-52. Someone delivered the sheet to Rollins.

A subsequent 58-42 victory over Baylor gave Kentucky its first NCAA championship. Kentucky won 34 games and lost two. Fourteen times it won by 30 points or more (three times by at least 54). Because it was an Olympic year, UK qualified for the Olympic Trials and easily advanced to the final against the Phillips Oilers, ostensibly amateurs but in reality the match of any professional team (the Oilers players worked for the oil company when not in uniform, a good deal in those days before every 6-foot-7 leaper made eight million dollars to turn pro out of high school).

The Oilers beat Kentucky 53-49. Barker's nose was broken early in the first half and he left the game, a circumstance Rupp used to explain the defeat. With Groza ineffective against the Oilers' 7-footer, Bob Kurland, Beard scored 23 points. "Beard is absolutely the best I ever saw," said Bud Browning, the Oilers coach. Rupp said he'd never

Did Lexington have a parade when Kentucky won its first NCAA championship in 1948? Any other silly questions?

Alex Groza was the Most Valuable Player in both the 1948 and 1949 NCAA tournaments won by UK. That's Alex with the trophy cradled in his arm.

seen a collegian play a finer game.

The UK and Oilers starting teams made up the Olympic squad and split playing time as the United States won eight straight games. Two pictures shared space on Beard's office wall 25 years later. One was UK's 1949 NCAA champions, the other was the 1948 U.S. Olympic team.

When Rollins graduated, Dale Barnstable, a junior, moved into Kentucky's lineup in '49, settling at forward with the conversion of Barker into a guard. Through its first 30 games, Kentucky lost only once — to defending NIT champion St. Louis — and won 14 games by 30 points or more. So merciless were Rupp's legions that they won six games by at least 42 points, and so talented were they that the brash idea of unprecedented victory in *both* the NIT and NCAA seemed a reasonable ambition.

But in the NIT's first round, all the betting favorites were beaten — Western Kentucky, Utah, St. Louis and Kentucky. Sports writers couldn't explain Kentucky's 67-56 loss to Loyola, a 10-point underdog. Kent Hollingsworth, writing in the UK school newspaper, said, "Kentucky came onto the floor and the whole team seemed to have adopted an air of indifference... Ralph Beard alone stood out for Kentucky. He hustled all the way...It was Beard who played his best when the going was tough." Hollingsworth criticized Groza's performance against Loyola's Jack Kerris, who outscored Groza 23-12. "Big Al didn't even attempt to block Kerris' pivot shot. He backed away and Kerris hooked them up there unmolested...On the offense, Groza wasn't himself. He didn't even try to get in front of Kerris...This defeat was no complicated plot, filled with intrigue...There are no excuses."

Basketball is a non-contact sport. Sure. Malcolm McMullen of Xavier puts some non-contact on Alex Groza's teeth.

Behind a Groza screen, Beard puts up a jump shot.

Groza, a three-time All-America, did not score a point in the second half. He took only three shots. "Kerris just whipped Groza," Beard said 26 years later. Beard had two points at halftime of that game, and Loyola led 32-31. With Groza getting nothing done and Wah-Wah Jones fouling out when UK had gained a 47-46 lead with 10 minutes to play, Beard was left alone to do UK's shooting. He wound up with 15 points. "It is inconceivable that three All-Americans should be off at the same time," Buck Weaver wrote in The Louisville Times. "But that was exactly the case. All three seemed dead on their feet." Larry Boeck of The Courier-Journal called it "basketball's most fantastic and dramatic upset . . . Few people here can believe yet what unfolded before their startled eyes . . . Groza played one of the poorest games of his career . . . Beard kept UK in the running." The date was March 14, 1949.

On March 27, UK won its second straight NCAA championship. Groza was the tournament hero. He scored 30 points in an 85-72 victory over Villanova, made 27 in a 76-47 rout of Illinois, and 25 in the 46-36 conquest of Oklahoma A&M

that moved Adolph Rupp to dance his impromptu jig.

More than 350 people showed up three weeks later for a testimonial dinner in Beard's honor at Louisville's Kentucky Hotel. The president of the Board of Aldermen, Dann Byck, set the tone: "We are here to pay tribute to a local boy who made good. We are here to admire him as more than an athlete, as a young man whose conduct has surpassed his ability as an All-American. The kids of this town and state hold him up as something special, as something more than a basketball, football and baseball star." Rupp attended the dinner. So did the state's acting governor and the chancellor of UK. "Words can't express my gratitude," said Beard, a young man whose future in the game he loved seemed unlimited.

He'd always played basketball. "His first basket was his potty chair," said Sue Beard, his mother. "He'd throw a little rubber ball at the chair. As he got older, he used the cutaway part of his high chair. Then we put a miniature basket over his bed. Then we tacked it up on the kitchen door. Finally we had to move it outside of Frank Beard, a prominent touring pro who made a million dollars playing golf but said he'd rather be "a real athlete, like Ralph.")

Life in Hardinsburg was simple. Whatever spending money Ralph had came from a newspaper route that brought in $2.50 a week (minus the 40 cents he paid his younger brother, Monie, to carry papers to Cotyville, four miles out of town). Mostly, Ralph played basketball, baseball and football. "Our front porch had four steps, and I'd play a baseball game by throwing a golf ball at the steps," Beard said. "I was the fielder. If I'd hit a corner with it, the ball would go over my head. That was a home run. If I caught it, it was an out. I'd play nine innings. Let me tell you, trying to catch that golf ball makes you quicker."

In 1941, Mrs. Beard moved to Louisville so Ralph could attend Male High. She was a guard at an aircraft plant for three years, changing shifts weekly. Later a supervisor of maids and a saleslady in a specialty shop, she earned free rent at 3rd and St. Catherine by cleaning six apartments and two sleeping rooms in two buildings. Ralph fired the furnaces every morning. The Beard apartment became the Male team's gathering place after games when Mrs. Beard, who played basketball as a girl in blouse and bloomers, cooked a big pot of chili.

Astonishingly successful in baseball, football and basketball — the country boy from Hardinsburg was a regular in all three sports as a junior, his second year at Male — Beard decided as a senior he'd like to be Male's first four-letter man in 25 years. So he won the half-mile run in the 1945 state meet, going the distance in 2:08.8. He also helped Male win its first state championship in basketball. The

The best amateur athlete in Kentucky in 1947. Beard receives a trophy from Joseph D. Scholtz of the Kentucky Amateur Athletic Union. Adolph Rupp watches.

in the yard."

Divorced when Ralph was 10 years old, Mrs. Beard worked as a stuffer of quilts and comforters in her mother-in-law's small business in Hardinsburg, a town of 900 people about 60 miles from Louisville. Beard's grandfather, Marvin Beard, had been a star track man and baseball player at Vanderbilt University. And the boy's father, Ralph Sr., played professional baseball with Evansville of the Three-I League. After the divorce, the elder Beard moved to Dallas, where in time he became a golf pro (and the father

Time out from baseball. Beard played professionally.

Ralph Beard, quarterback. As a freshman at Kentucky, Beard started three games at fullback behind quarterback George Blanda. When he hurt a shoulder, Beard quit football.

recruiters knew about him. Georgia wanted him for football. Auburn, Vanderbilt, Southern Methodist and Georgia Tech asked him to come visit. He went to Ohio State and Notre Dame. The coach at Tennessee, Johnny Mauer, was especially anxious to land Beard. But Kentucky owned his heart. "I'd always read about UK, and I never wanted to go anyplace else," Beard said.

It wasn't quite that cut-and-dried. As a member of the Kentucky All-Star team in the summer series with Indiana, Beard worked out at Western Kentucky under coach Ed Diddle. "We had two-a-day workouts, we ate all we wanted, we swam in the pool and I thought, 'This is heaven,'" Beard said. "Wah Jones and I contemplated going to Western. Coach Diddle made us feel like we were his sons. It was a super week." For Ralph Beard, who sometimes borrowed money so he could eat lunch at Male, this was his first taste of the good life. All because he could play basketball.

If an anvil-footed playmaker from Illinois was too young to know about Ralph Beard at his best, a few days in the

105

library cured that ignorance. "You were *good*!" the playmaker said, and "Rapid Ralph," as he was called, pointed to a picture on his family room wall. It showed Beard, Groza, Ed Macauley, Bob Davies and George Mikan, the All-NBA team of 1951. "Hey, the five best in the *world*," Beard said.

Beard and Groza played for the Indianapolis Olympians — so named because the majority stockholders were Beard, Groza, Jones, Barker, Joe Holland (also an ex-UK player) and Babe Kimbrough, a former Lexington sports writer who first proposed the Kentuckians go into the basketball business for themselves, an unprecedented endeavor (and never again done). As rookies in the 1949-50 season, Beard scored 14.9 points a game and Groza 23.4 to lead Indianapolis to a first-place finish in the NBA's Western Division. The Olympians were eliminated in the second round of playoffs.

The next season, Beard scored 16.8 points a game, eighth best in the league, immediately ahead of a rookie named Bob Cousy. By then Beard had decided basketball was his future. He'd played a year of pro baseball, too, and given it up although he was considered a major league prospect as an infielder. "I planned to play pro basketball until my legs fell off," Beard said. "I was only 22 and I never played better basketball in my life." The Olympians, slumping, finished fourth in their division that year.

Financially, the team was successful. Each of the six owners was paid $5,000 in salary and a $5,000 bonus both years. "We had $27,000 in the bank and had paid all the debts," Beard said 25 years later. "Nowadays that's small potatoes, but back then that was flying pretty high."

In the summer of 1951, the national per-capita income was $3,229. A Gallup poll said Americans favored a large-scale defense program 7-1 no matter the outcome of the Korean peace talks. Accordionist Dick Contino was taken to jail for two weeks, punishment for trying to dodge the draft. The Yankees led Boston by a few percentage points in the American League baseball race, and the Dodgers were nine games ahead of the Giants. In Louisville, a youngster named Mickey Mantle went 1-for-5 in the Kansas City Blues' 10-8 victory over the Colonels at Parkway Field. All that was reported on July 25, 1951, in The Courier-Journal, which also carried a Page One picture of a New York gambler who admitted bribing Bradley University basketball players to fix games. The picture showed Nick Englisis covering his face with his hands.

Three weeks later, Adolph Rupp, who said he had never seen Englisis around his basketball players, delivered his 10-foot pole speech. And on Oct. 15 the coach made a plea for leniency before the Chicago Quarterback Club. "The Chicago Black Sox threw games — but these kids only shaved points." Later, Rupp would say he didn't know then what was coming the night of Oct. 19.

Beard, Groza, Jones and Holland, en route to Moline, Ill., for an exhibition game in preparation for the NBA season beginning two weeks later, stopped at Chicago Stadium to watch the pro champion Rochester Royals play the College All-Stars, coached by Rupp. At 3 a.m. the next morning, Willie Barnstable, the wife of Dale Barnstable, woke Sue Beard with a telephone call.

"Something awful's happened to Dale and Ralph," Mrs. Barnstable said.

"What? What happened?" Mrs. Beard said. "A car wreck?"

"Worse," said Mrs. Barnstable.

As Beard and Groza left Chicago Stadium, Lt. James Oakey, head of the Illinois state's attorney's police, and Thomas McInerney, chief investigator for the state's attorney, approached the players and said, "Come on, we're going to the Cook County DA's office and you're under arrest."

Under questioning that would continue seven hours through the night, Beard and Groza first denied any part in "fixing" games. Never had they taken money, they said, to shave points; nor had they conspired with gamblers to go over the bookies' point spread. Finally, the players confessed when confronted by a witness for the district attorney: Nick Englisis.

Three times the UK All-Americas were paid for going over the point spread. The pay: $100 a night. For being under the spread in the NIT against Loyola, Beard, Groza and Barnstable received $500 each. That was the deal for the Tennessee game at Lexington a month earlier, too. The payoff was made by a gambler named Nat (Lovey) Brown in Groza's car under a viaduct. Beard's admitted take from the gamblers was $1,300 for five games. "I'm so mixed up," Beard said three days after his arrest. "I wish I knew why I did it. I've been asking myself and it doesn't make sense. The money was nothing."

Barnstable was the basketball coach at Louisville Manual High, successful in his first year with a 30-3 record and advancement to the semifinals of the State Tournament. He was arrested at home at 2 o'clock in the morning, taken from his wife and five-month-old twin daughters by five officers. "We just didn't think, I guess," Barnstable said that week. "If just somebody who had suspected what was going on at Madison Square Garden had come up and told us that point shaving or things like that were against the law, we'd never have done it.

"Do you think we'd have jeopardized our careers — Al and Ralph, particularly, who knew they had great pro prospects — for a measly $700 or so each?

"These guys were smooth talkers. Take you out for a stroll and treat you and before you know it, you're into it. They point out they're not asking you to dump the game, just to pick up a few bucks by shaving a few points, but still winning and nobody getting hurt except the gamblers. And they'd ask what's wrong with going over the limit.

"...But I'll tell you this — if those guys had offered us $10,000 or $20,000 or $30,000 to throw a game, we'd have thrown them out of the hotel window.

"You take some money for winning games, you don't know exactly what's going on, and the next thing you know, you are in it deep — too deep."

The night he was arrested at Chicago Stadium, Ralph Beard, 22, not long removed from Hardinsburg, still much the same boy who pedaled a bicycle to deliver newspapers, was put in Cook County Jail with prisoners he would describe as "psychos and winos." He was in custody 15 hours and when released he flew to Indianapolis, where he was driven to Louisville by his mother. As they opened the door to the apartment building at 3rd and St. Catherine, Beard said, "Mom, aren't you ashamed to walk in with me?" Sue Beard said, "I've never been ashamed of you, and I never will be."

Beard and Groza with detectives.

Seven months after their arrest, General Sessions Judge Saul S. Streit of New York City suspended sentence on the three UK players. Each pleaded guilty to conspiring with gamblers to shave points, a misdemeanor punishable by a term up to three years in the city penitentiary. Streit said his leniency was prompted by the players' full cooperation. That cooperation, however, did Beard and Groza no good when it came to playing basketball again.

The NBA, which already had suspended the stars, then forced Beard and Groza to sell their shares of the Indianapolis Olympians. Stock worth $10,000 a year earlier brought the players $1,000. Under terms of a three-year probation set up by Judge Streit, the All-NBA players, two of the five best in the world, could not play basketball anywhere. When they tried to form a team in a minor league, Streit sent Beard a telegram. "He said if I so much as touched a basketball in a YMCA, he'd put my ass in jail," Beard said.

Judge Streit leveled a withering attack at Adolph Rupp, accusing the coach of everything except The Great Train Robbery. "The undisputed facts," the judge said, "are that he aided and abetted in the immoral subsidization of the players. With his knowledge, the charges in his care were openly exploited, their physical welfare was neglected, and he utterly failed to build their characters or instill any morals — indeed if he did not impair them." Football and basketball at Kentucky, the judge said, "have been highly systematized and commercialized enterprises; (there has been) covert subsidization of players, ruthless exploitation of athletes, cribbing at examinations, 'illegal' recruiting, a reckless disregard of their physical welfare, matriculation of unqualified students, demoralization of athletes by the coach, alumni and townspeople and the most flagrant abuse of the 'athletic scholarship.' . . ." Judge Streit's outrage at Big Time athletics was so absolute that he proposed state laws to make it a crime to award athletic scholarships.

Such laws were never passed.

Streit may have found the facts "undisputed," but Kentuckians disputed them passionately. A statement signed by Gov. Lawrence Wetherby and UK president Herman L. Donovan said the judge "went to unnecessary lengths in blackening the reputation" of UK. Streit had mixed fact and opinion, the statement said, to produce "a distorted and untrue" picture of Kentucky's athletic programs.

"For what has happened (the statement said) in respect to basketball, the administrative officials and the athletics staff are partially responsible and they are ready to acknowledge that responsibility.

"But the blame for the tragic events . . . must be shared by the public that persists in gambling and in protecting gamblers, by overzealous alumni, real and synthetic, who place athletics victories above all other considerations, by radio stations, newspapers and magazines that have featured college sports out of all proportion to their importance, and by college and university administrative officials and coaches throughout the land."

At an alumni meeting, President Donovan said Streit's statement was "an harangue filled with misrepresentation . . . The judge forgot that Madison Square Garden was in his bailiwick and that place is one of the rottenest gambling joints in the world. All the culprits were in Kentucky — according to Judge Streit."

Donovan said the UK players in the scandal "essentially are not dishonorable — they were taken in by slick gamblers . . . They have been held up to scorn by the court and by the light of far more publicity than usually is given a man who commits murder or some more heinous crime."

Apparently Rupp met his match in bombastics in the robed person of Saul Streit, for the coach had only one response to the judge's accusations. "I am willing for the citizens of Kentucky to be the judge," Rupp said. Later, the coach said he favored "de-emphasizing de-emphasis . . . I'm a little tired of this de-emphasis business. Do they want de-emphasis on ability in sports, spectator interest or on winning games?"

Subsequent investigations by the Southeastern Conference and the NCAA, prompted by Streit's action, brought about the suspension of UK's basketball team for the 1952-53 season. But president Donovan, under pressure from SEC schools to fire Rupp, refused. "Coach Rupp is an honorable man who did not knowingly violate athletic rules," Donovan said.

What Rupp admitted to was giving his basketball players $50 apiece after the Sugar Bowl tournament games of 1950. At the time, the SEC approved gifts of $250 to football players in bowl games and UK decided that was a good idea for basketball "bowl" games, too. Only, the SEC rules said no. Rupp also admitted knowing that Lexington merchants provided suits of clothes for his players, and he never denied Streit's charge that he gave players from $5 to $50 for games well played. (Asked during testimony to a grand jury if Rupp were so generous in defeat, Barnstable said, "No, sir, you were lucky to get something to eat then.")

Dr. Donovan, defending Rupp, said UK was guilty — but no more so than any team in the SEC, and to fire his basketball coach would be to admit to greater sin. Neither did the point-shaving scandals worry Rupp. "There was no chance they'd fire me," Rupp said two decades later. "The board of trustees told me, 'Adolph, you didn't know a damn thing about the fix.' We were beating every team in the nation, so why should I be suspicious? I never entertained the thought we were involved in the fix."

The hassles made Rupp a coach without mercy. "Those other SEC schools, in order to win, said, 'Get rid of that s.o.b. Rupp,'" he said. "That made me more determined than ever that, by gawd, I was going to have great teams here at the university. I said I'd get rid of all those SEC coaches who voted against me, and, by gawd, I got rid of every coach that was in on it. There have been 56 coaches in the conference from the time I came in until I left. I survived all of them." He also survived a lawyer, J. A. Edge of Lexington, who filed a $500,000 lawsuit in 1952 claiming Rupp conspired with Ed Curd, the Lexington bookmaker, and infamous New York gambler Frank Costello in a "debasing scheme of gambling in schools, colleges, and university sports and athletics." The suit was dismissed quickly in U.S. District Court by Judge H. Church Ford, who said it was filed only "to gain notoriety." The lawyer Edge, suspended from practice for a year as a result, said of Rupp, "You cannot escape the idea that something was between this man and the others . . . why doesn't he (Rupp) say he never sold those points? Why doesn't he say he has no connections? Why does he stay on when the boys have to leave? . . . He just can't walk out because he is a coach. He has made nothing but a mere informal denial." The date was April 15, 1953.

On September 17, 1953, Marilyn Beard, 1424 Falcon Drive, Louisville, filed a Circuit Court suit asking for divorce from Ralph Beard. The suit prepared by attorney Laura Miller Derry charged cruelty. Mrs. Beard, once a West Virginia beauty queen, asked custody of the couple's child, Ralph Beard III, then 3 years old. The Beards were married July 16, 1949, at Morgantown, W. Va.

Beard's life had disintegrated in the 23 months since he walked out of Chicago Stadium. By order of Judge Streit, Beard could not play basketball anywhere. Professional baseball also turned him away. He moved from job to job in Louisville, laying pipe, selling cars. "I drifted. It was a void." Beard spoke of himself in the second person: "You look on yourself as a complete failure. You had blown the whole thing. You wanted to go away and die." He didn't blame his wife for wanting out. "I was an absolutely unbearable person to live with." Was he mad at the world? Full of self pity? "All of that. Everything. I was a complete void." Second person again: "But you don't die. You realize, finally, you can't die."

Betty Scott "got my head on straight," Beard said. He had known her brother, so had called Betty for a date in 1954. "She was just very level-headed. She said you can't go through life mourning that mistake. You've got to live." They were married March 18, 1955 — and Beard was drafted into the Army in July, 1955 — at age 27. The Streit probation period was over by then, and Beard starred for the Camp Zama (Japan) basketball team. Back in Louisville in 1957, he sold cars for Koster-Swope Buick. He saw no future there, so he went to all the employment agencies in town. Soon he had a sales job with Bristol Laboratories, peddling pharmaceutical supplies. In December of 1958, he left Bristol to work for one of his customers, Gould's Division of Kauffman-Lattimer Co., a pharmaceutical wholesaler. Beard began selling on the road, and in 1973 became general manager of Gould's.

He sat at his desk. Correspondence and manila folders were arranged in neat piles. Beard's office was without frill, as purposeful as its occupant. A portrait of Ralph Beard at age 47 would show him as he was at 17. Lean. Intense. So vital, so full of passion, that even sitting he seemed to be in motion. The only difference detectable was that Beard, the executive, was not flying for a layup.

"The scandal broke Oct. 20, 1951, and I haven't ever forgotten it, and I won't ever forget it until they hit me in the face with that first spade full of dirt," he said. For an hour Beard had talked about his life, the conversation moving relentlessly toward Chicago Stadium. He knew it. "You are going to mention it — the scandal — aren't you?" Beard said to a man taking notes for a book. "It's as much a part of my life as anything else.

"At 23, basketball was the only thing I was interested in. I was going to play forever. And I was pretty close with a buck. I was going to set up my own business. Then, the scandal. At 23, it was like taking a wooden dagger and putting it in a vampire's heart. I figured the world was over. You could stick a fork in me, I was done." Beard looked around his office and smiled. "Of course, I wasn't."

Beard raised his voice. "I'll tell you the same thing I told the assistant district attorney in New York the first time I ever met him: If it was wrong to take the money, I did wrong. I took the money. But *never*, and I'll swear on my mother's eyes, I *never* did anything to influence any basketball game, either above or below the point spread."

Beard spoke rapidly and in incomplete sentences: "Yes, I took the money, but as God is my judge . . . Only two people know the truth, me and the good Lord . . . People will say, 'Yeah, that lying s.o.b. is probably the biggest crook on earth' . . . People can either believe it or not, but this is the truth — I had never did anything to influence the score of a basketball game. I had too much pride in my basketball to do that . . . Then *why* take the money? Because of ingrained insecurity from my childhood . . . Well, they'll say there are millions of poor people and they don't take money . . . Well, maybe they weren't exposed to it."

Beard said his son, Scott, born nine years after the scandal, read his scrapbooks. "He sees the good and the bad. It's all there. I saved the good, why not the bad? He's asked, 'Hey, Dad, what about this?' I said, 'Son, I did wrong.' And I've paid more than most people paid. Because I paid with my life."

Did Beard ever think of what might have been? An Indianapolis team in the NBA for 25 years would have made millionaires of its owners.

"Oh, *yes*! I have often thought about that. Some of these days when I'm working from 8 in the morning til 10:30 at night, with customers coming in — yes, I think about it, all the time."

The worst time was winter. "In the summer, I never think about the scandal. I play golf, hit shag balls with my son. When it gets to be basketball season, though, it comes back. I have nightmares about it. Just as vivid as if it was happening today."

Ralph Beard took a tarnished gold trophy from a shelf in his family room. He lived in a ranch-style house in a neighborhood of $50,000 homes in eastern Louisville. Pictures of Beard and plaques attesting his ability were on a wall under the trophies. "This one is for Player of the Year in the Garden," Beard said. His wife, Betty, laughed. "Don't get any more down," she said. "I don't dust up there but twice a year."

Typical suburbia. The father in golf shorts. The mother in a golf skirt. Nice house, comfortable life. The Beard's daughter, Jill, 18, was a freshman at UK. Beard's son by his first marriage, Mike, 25, lived in Pittsburgh and sold computers. He often visited Louisville. This was a summer day, and the Beards spoke proudly of Scott, 14, the youngest qualifier in the Kentucky State Amateur golf tournament.

"I took a day of vacation to take Scott down to Lexington for a practice round," Beard said. "I wanted to play with him, but they wouldn't allow it. So I walked the course with him."

"How'd he do?" Mrs. Beard said.

"Hey, he shot 79. Not bad. The golf course is not going to overpower him. The par-fours are 445 yards, 435 and 420. He'll have to get that wedge in there and make a putt. Hey, he's so *excited*! He's practically *running* after the ball to hit it. I wouldn't have missed it for the world. This may have been the greatest day of my life, to see Scott pumped up like that."

"Excited, huh?" somebody said.

"Oh, man, is he *ever*! He's so full of himself. That's what it takes to be a champion. That *overpowering* desire. Desire that won't let you be anything but."

"How'd Scott do when you left him at the motel?" Mrs. Beard said. It was the young man's first time alone away from home.

"Hey, I got him bologna and bread and cheese and cherry pies and Twinkies," Beard said. A smile played at the corners of his mouth and he spoke hurriedly, the words bursting into the air. "We watched the U.S. Open on television, and it got to be 6 o'clock. I figure everything is all right. So I start to leave. And quick as that, Scott says, 'Don't go, Dad.'

"About broke my heart. 'Don't go, Dad.'" Beard slapped his palm on his leg and laughed. "Shot a 79 on that tough golf course." Then Ralph Beard leaned back and said, "I'd like to go through this day again."

The Fabulous Five, 1964. From left are Ralph Beard, Kenny Rollins, Cliff Barker, Wah-Wah Jones and Alex Groza.

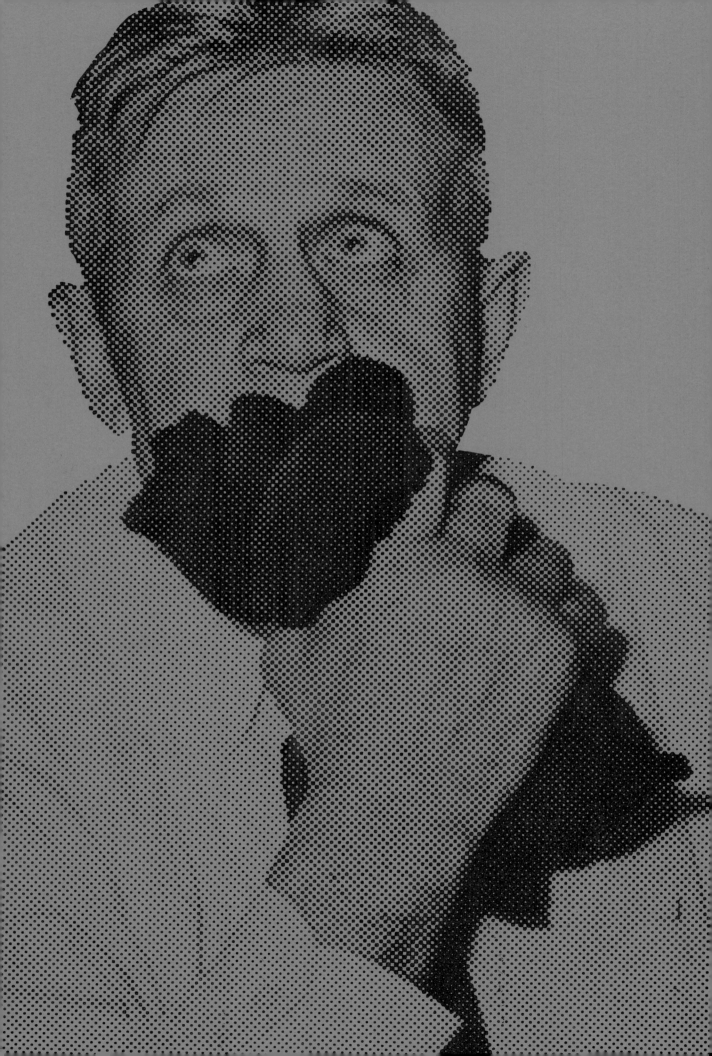

THE MAN WITH THE RED TOWEL

No heart was so hard as to refuse admittance to Ed Diddle. It was extraordinary that in a small state like Kentucky two college basketball coaches would gain everlasting fame. In his khakis, Adolph Rupp sent teams to war with instructions to take no prisoners. He was Gen. Patton with a whistle. Doing it Rupp's way, no matter how much the players hated him, they made it safely through the war/game, for which they gave thanks if not love. Only 150 miles away in Bowling Green, Rupp's contemporary, Ed Diddle, made Western Kentucky a power of such strength that when he died in 1970 UK and Western ranked 1-2 nationally in all-time victories. Diddle was no creampuff. He scolded Dero Downing: "What makes you think you're such a good basketball player? I found you up there at Horse Cave, just milking a little Jersey cow, and you're not much better now than you were then, and all you know is what I've taught you." Downing, later the president of the university, said, "Then, when you felt the lowest, like you weren't worth killing, he'd pat you on the rear — and you felt like you could beat the world." With Ed Did-

dle, the pats outnumbered the scolds, and with the victories came affection.

It was easy to like Diddle. Rupp was steel — cold and unbending. Even the percussion of his name was foreboding. But Diddle's was a name from a Mother Goose rhyme. His eyes were large and sad, as if borrowed from a beagle, and he parted his hair in the middle. Eternally unsuccessful in attempts to diet, largely because he ate three or four breakfasts on a daily conversation tour of Bowling Green restaurants, Diddle was a six-footer who sometimes weighed 240 pounds. He was guileless and innocent, a man with a child's heart. Only hidebound grammarians could have thought ill of Ed Diddle. The coach used words never before heard, and he spoke sentences upside down. "His mind was faster than his tongue," said Kelly Thompson, who stayed in school at Western with the help of a $25 loan co-signed by Diddle and in time became the university president. "But he was never self-conscious about it. He laughed at what he said, too."

Dressing down Red McCrocklin, an All-America, the coach said, "The trouble

Ed Diddle, 1955.

116

with you, Red, is that you're too inde-damn-pendent." He showed a prospect around campus, pointing out the "pussy-footwillow." He would scream if a player threw a "louse pass," and to lose badly at cards was to be "hog-swallowed."

On a recruiting trip to Tennessee with assistant coach Ted Hornback, Diddle had been asleep about five hours. When he woke, Diddle said, "Ted, let's stop here and eat. If I don't get some sleep soon, I'm going to starve to death." He'd been asleep in Thompson's car driving to Danville when he sat up and saw city lights. "Are we on this side of town, or the other side?" Diddle said.

Exasperated because McCrocklin insisted on running around the outside of a screen instead of going directly to the basket, Diddle stopped practice. "Red, do you know anything about physics?" he said. "A little," McCrocklin said. And Diddle said, "Then what's the straightest point between two lines?"

Numbers tried the coach's tongue sorely. A spectator at practice watched Curly Ellis make several shots from the pivot and said, "Coach, Curly can hit a million from that point." "A million?" Diddle said. "My gosh, he could hit a thousand!" He was in awe of Fred Sawyer, the Louisville center. "That Sawyer is the biggest man I ever saw. Why, he must be 6 feet 13 or 14, at least."

Getting ready to play Louisville in 1950, Diddle was worried. "Oh, my. Oh, my! That team always plays better against us than they do any other team. They play 100 per cent better. We'll be lucky to beat them by a half a point."

"By half a point?" somebody said.

"Maybe I'm being overconfident," Diddle said. "I'll settle for less than half a point."

An ambidextrous player became "amphibious." Players were told to line up "alphabetically according to height." When tape was scarce, Diddle declared, "We're the usingest tape team in the country." He introduced his son, Ed Jr., and said, "He's about as big as I was when I was his size." Retire? "I intend to die at Western with my feet on."

Diddle coached baseball, too. Western was to play at Eastern Kentucky, 200 miles away in Richmond. "We'll have to cancel the game," Diddle said over the telephone. "It's raining." The Eastern Kentucky coach said he hadn't seen any rain all day. "Well, just look out your window," Diddle said.

Then there was Rex.

Rex was an Irish Setter of many talents. Not only was he Diddle's hunting dog, Rex shagged foul balls at baseball practice, too, dropping them at the feet of the catcher. "Everyone in school was fond of Rex," Diddle said. "He'd go in the class room and sit there on his haunches, never moving until class was over." So it was a campus-wide emergency when Rex disappeared. For three or four days, the search went on. Then Diddle had a flat tire and opened his car trunk to get the jack. There was Rex, where his master put him in preparation for a forgotten hunting trip. "Rex, you old dog," Diddle said, "where have you been all this time?"

In 42 seasons at Western Kentucky, Diddle's teams won 32 conference championships. They played in three NCAA tournaments and eight NIT's (from 1942 to 1954, when the NIT was king of the hill). Eighteen times Diddle's teams won more than 20 games in a season, doing it 10 straight years from 1934 on. His 1936 team was the first from the South in the on a December night in 1922, to beat the Adairville Independents 103-7. Diddle ran across campus to report the astounding score to Dr. H. H. Cherry, the school president who had hired him three months earlier. "We play the fast break because it makes people come to our gymnasium," the coach said later. "They like to see scoring. We give them what they like. I see it as entertainment." To add pizzazz, Diddle painted basketballs red and white, the school's colors, for use in warmup drills. And he encouraged his players to dunk the ball, a piece of show-offery frowned upon by conventional coaches.

No testimony praised Diddle for his defensive genius. His best team may have been the 1948-49 outfit that ranked No. 3 in the country while Kentucky was No. 1. After an 83-58 victory over Long Island that season, a New York sports writer called Western "a bunch of lanky guys with pogo sticks for legs who aren't too concerned with defense." Basketball was a simple game, Diddle said. "The boys come out, you give them a ball and point to the basket. 'Put it through there, you tell them, and that's all there is to it — almost." The word "defense" may not have been in Ed Diddle's revisionistic dictionary.

He was tough in practice. "You had to have your shirttail in," said Dee Gibson. "You never took a shot you wouldn't take in a game. There was no nonchalance at all in running plays. It had to be perfect execution to please Mr. Diddle. And he didn't even want you to whisper to anybody. 'We don't have time to whisper,' he said. And there was no drinking of water."

Diddle valued victory. "Don't ever think he was a pushover," Kelly Thomp-

When Western Kentucky upset Louisville 86-77 in the 1955 Kentucky Invitational Tournament, some of Diddle's former players joined in the backslapping.

Olympic Trials. Western won 759 games for Diddle, lost 302. Various All-America lists carried 13 of his players: Red Mc-Crocklin, Carlyle Towery, Oran Mc-Kinney, Dee Gibson, Don (Duck) Ray, Odie Spears, Johnny Oldham, Bob Lavoy, Rip Gish, Art Spoelstra, Tom Marshall, Bobby Rascoe and Darel Carrier. Like Rupp, Diddle was a member of the Naismith Memorial Hall of Fame.

Ed Diddle needed only one game to demonstrate his idea of college basketball. Young, strong and ambitious, Diddle allowed his first Western Kentucky team,

Movie cowboy Gene Autry with the coach.

son said. "He'd fight like a bobcat. There was nothing he ever feared. He had this great heart, accompanied by this aggressive competitive spirit. Second-best was nothing to him." In 1959, in the 37th year of his coaching career, Diddle yet was zealous in pursuit of first-best. "If you play the game right, you're gonna win," he said then. "And if you don't win, you're in trouble. Real bad, awful trouble! If there's anything I can't stand, it's a happy loser."

The best way to avoid the calamity of defeat was to get good players. Diddle had a formula. "When I'm scouting players, I look for tall boys, up over 6-3, with big hands and big feet. If they haven't got big feet, they'll fall down . . . They've got to be tough and lean and weigh up close to 200 pounds. . . . I don't want any boys with fat on their hips. Those kind can't run and they're apt to stand around and think out there. I want the nervous kind, the kind with temperament and brains, like a race horse."

He wanted one thing more, too. "A pretty good athlete who is a competitor will beat a talented boy who has a faint heart everytime. The thing I always looked for first in a boy was his fire. We can develop his talents, but only God can give him his fire."

That fire warmed Ed Diddle early. At age 64 he said, "Ever since I shot my first basket on an outdoor court in Adair County 56 years ago, I wanted to spend the rest of my life with this game." One of five sons of John and Mary Elizabeth Diddle, he grew up on a farm near Gradyville, Ky., and went to school in Columbia. Always a good athlete, he played both football and basketball at Centre College, whose teams then were the best in the

Centre College's team of 1918-1919: Bo McMillin, left front; Ed Diddle, next; John Sherman Cooper, right back.

state. "The first football game I ever saw, I played in," Diddle said. "It was mighty rough. I didn't know the rules too good, and I clipped a lot. I almost killed everybody on that Marshall team. I learned a lot that first game." Ed Diddle's nickname at Centre was "Mule," an earned tribute to his strength and persistence.

The campus at Danville in 1919 was a gathering place for rising stars. The football coach was Uncle Charlie Moran, whose Praying Colonels two years later would amaze the nation by bringing down haughty Harvard 6-0. The hero of that game would be Alvin (Bo) McMillin, a running back who once profited from the destructive blocking of Mule Diddle. The 1919 basketball team, with Diddle the center and leading scorer, was undefeated in 11 games and hailed as the best in the South. Diddle's playmates included John Sherman Cooper, later a distinguished U.S. Senator, and the football players Red Roberts, Madison Bell and McMillin. "Bo didn't shoot the ball at the basket," Diddle said. "He attacked the basket with the ball. But before he was through, he was a pretty fair player, I guarantee you."

They gave no athletic scholarships then, so Diddle waited on tables and washed dishes for 60 boarders three times a day at Mrs. Rice's place. He also fired the water heater and swept the gymnasium floor. Other players, to get some spending money, sold game tickets the school had given them. Diddle preferred to give the tickets to somebody who couldn't afford to buy them. That's how he came to be a coach. Kelly Thompson told the story:

"It was in 1920, the summer after Mr. Diddle had graduated from Centre. He was out West, somewhere in Colorado, working for the White-Myers Chautauqua Company, making $18 a week. He'd filled in part-time as coach at Monticello that last winter, but he didn't know what he was going to do when the summer ended. He didn't have a job and he hadn't saved any money. Then he got this telegram from Dr. Smock."

Dr. Ben Wilson Smock then was president of the Muhlenburg County Board of Education.

"Mr. Diddle couldn't place the name. But, finally, he remembered. Dr. Smock had been a medical student at the University of Louisville. He came down to Lexington to see Centre play Kentucky a football game. But he didn't have any tickets.

". . . So Mr. Diddle ran into Dr. Smock, whom he'd never seen before, and gave him the tickets. Dr. Smock told him later that if he hadn't given him the tickets, he wouldn't have been able to buy his girl anything to eat that night.

"Anyway, two or three years later, Dr. Smock sent the telegram to Mr. Diddle. The telegram said: 'Vacancy in coaching position at Greenville High School. Would you accept job, and if so, at what salary?

"Well, Mr. Diddle answered him: 'I will accept the job. And to hell with the salary.'"

In his second season at Greenville, 1922, Diddle had a fine basketball team with a 26-2 record when it came time to travel to Owensboro for the regional tournament. Mother Nature butted in, and Ed Diddle was on his way to Western Kentucky. Kelly Thompson again:

"Greenville couldn't get to Owensboro because the Green River flooded and the ferry was closed. So Mr. Diddle called the state athletic association, and they switched the game to Bowling Green. Well, Greenville upset a couple ball teams and everybody was so impressed with the fire and thunder of that basketball team — especially in the coach — that Western hired Diddle."

The Western president then was Dr. H. H. Cherry, who had split rails and peddled apples to pay his way through the Southern Normal and Business College in Bowling Green. Eventually he became president of that school, and kept the job when it entered the state system as Western Kentucky State Normal and

Teachers College. He thought of the campus as his home. His wrath was not provoked easily, but he did not long abide anyone who bothered the squirrels or violated the flowers on campus. Neither did he brook any fun-poking at the Reserve Officers Training Corps (ROTC). Diddle became Cherry's protege, and soon enough he too was protective of Western. He stopped students on campus who wore high school letter jackets to remind them they were part of Western and could leave the offending jacket at home. Perhaps the only recorded instance of Diddle behaving less than fatherly was his abrupt collaring of a fellow whose mistake it was to snicker at marching ROTC cadets. "If anybody is responsible for the family-type atmosphere at Western Kentucky," Kelly Thompson said, "it is Dr. Cherry first and Mr. Diddle second."

The Western Kentucky coaching job was no prize. Diddle's salary was $150 a month, $100 less than he made at Greenville. The school's basketball history was a giggle. For 28 games in three seasons, records show only 12 scores. The team played its games in a barn said to seat 250. To be certain Diddle worked for his $150, Western assigned him to coach football, baseball and girls basketball. (Diddle soon earned a bonus. He married his All-State forward, Margaret Louise Monin, who had helped Western win a state championship over UK girls coached by Albert Benjamin Chandler, later Governor and U.S. Senator.)

It was a dozen years before Western had a 20-victory season. But by then the school had built a new basketball place called the Big Red Barn, with seats for 4,500 customers, and Diddle sustained the enthusiasm with teams that from 1934 to 1943 won 250 games and lost only 41. In this decade that saw Western rise to national prominence, Diddle established clear superiority over the state's other regional universities. Western was 11-1 against Morehead State, 23-9 against Murray State and 20-2 against Eastern Kentucky.

"Diddle had a helluva thing going at Bowling Green," Paul McBrayer said. "You couldn't hardly win down there. Western led us 17-13 once with five minutes left in the first half — and by halftime they were ahead 42-21. It was something unbelievable. We had one good player foul out, and a Western player hit another one. Diddle had everybody brainwashed. After that one, I told him that from then on, any time Eastern played Western, it would be a state of war."

McBrayer was Eastern Kentucky's coach from 1946 to mid-season in 1962, winning 214 games, losing 141. An All-America guard for coach Johnny Mauer at Kentucky in 1930, McBrayer coached at Kavanaugh High School before return-

Squeezed in, 5,500 people came to Western's Big Red Barn for a 1948 game with Bowling Green University.

ing to UK as an assistant to the young Adolph Rupp in 1934. He stayed nine seasons, went off to war and came back to coach Eastern Kentucky, then playing a small-college schedule.

"In two years we were in the university division — in spite of the administration, which wanted to stay small-time," McBrayer said. "I was either going to move it out of there — or move myself."

Thanks to exceptional players such as Jack Adams ("the best competitor since Ty Cobb"), Jim Baechtold, Chuck Mrazovich, Bob Mulcahy, Carl Cole, Larry Wood and Elmer Tolson, McBrayer moved Eastern quickly. In 1948, Eastern once was ranked among the top 10 teams in the country. One of its victories was over Western Kentucky's great team — a 42-40 upset at Bowling Green. That would be the *only* victory McBrayer ever won on Diddle's floor in 15 tries.

By 1960, in fact, Eastern had lost 10 straight times at Bowling Green, which did nothing to improve McBrayer's customary dour opinion of the cursed Hilltoppers. And things went to a warm place in a handbasket the night of February 16.

Paul McBrayer, All-America at Kentucky, 1930.

Western's Bobby Rascoe drove for a layup. He was fouled by Eastern Kentucky's Ralph Richardson, and the two of them hurtled into the Western bench, directly under the basket.

It happened in the first half with about three minutes before intermission. It was a big game, with the conference championship at stake. Earlier, Eastern had beaten Western 80-73 at Richmond. But this night, Western led 38-20 when Rascoe and Richardson fell into Ed Diddle's lap. Protecting himself, the old coach shoved them away.

Or did Diddle abuse the Eastern player?

"He was trying to attack my boy when he had done absolutely nothing out of the way," McBrayer said of Diddle.

So McBrayer took his team off the court.

He refused to play any more.

Eastern forfeited the game — and the championship.

McBrayer's teams accomplished good things. Eastern ended Western's 21-game victory streak in 1954 when Diddle's boys were ranked No. 3 in the nation. Eastern beat Louisville a week before Louisville won the 1956 NIT. In 14 Ohio Valley Conference seasons under McBrayer, Eastern won three league championships. But . . .

But always, forever, maybe even in his sleep, McBrayer was being beaten by Western Kentucky. Six times — count 'em — Eastern finished second to Western in the OVC. McBrayer won only 11 of 38 games against Diddle. He resigned in midseason of 1962 — immediately after losing to Western 96-92 at Richmond. McBrayer said his health was poor.

Only those with iron will and strong

McBrayer, Eastern Kentucky coach, 1955.

heart survive in the Ohio Valley Conference. With Western, Eastern, Murray State and Morehead State as members from the beginning in 1948, the OVC became basketball's Hatfield-McCoy number. To confess admiration for an opponent was to risk confinement in a dark place. Maybe in some places basketball was a game. In Bowling Green, Richmond, Morehead and Murray, it was, in the words of the former Murray State coach Cal Luther, "an emotional binge." Luther said, "I've often wondered what an enterprising fellow could steal during one of our home games. The whole city police force attends the games, along with half of the state police. I'm aware of this because most of them call me for tickets and I oblige where I can because it never hurts to be friends with the law." Life in the OVC, Luther decided after 14 seasons, was "pure hell."

Adron Doran, then president of Morehead State and husband of Mignon, who played the organ at home games in a roller-rinkish, 5,000-seat arena, once stalked an official *on* the court *during* a game. (A photographer made pictures of the happening; Doran caused the film to be confiscated and exposed.) Struck in the face by thrown ice, Western Kentucky athletic director Johnny Oldham, Diddle's successor as coach, said he wasn't going back to Morehead anymore. Why? "Because I've been there," Oldham said.

At Eastern, the game clock went haywire with 10 seconds to play and Murray State lost by two points. Then at Bowling Green, Western scored in the last second to beat Murray. Luther sprinted from his bench and "congratulated" the timekeeper, William (Big Six) Henderson, with a handshake, saying, "Nice game, Six." Later Henderson, in a red vest, shared a Coke with Oldham in the winning coach's office. Luther said, "Murray plays 40-minute games in this crazy league — 39 minutes and 50 seconds here, 40 minutes and 10 seconds there." The next season, Luther took his team off the floor with 11 seconds to play against Eastern. He had a seven-point lead.

In 1952 Morehead State and Tennessee Tech began a game at 8:15 p.m. It ended at 10:45. In legend this was "The Night the Clock Stood Still." The Tennessee Tech timepiece was suffering a bad case of the slows, and the teams played 60 minutes of basketball, not 40. Eight Morehead players fouled out, leaving only four on the court. Resourceful coach Ellis Johnson, the old Ashland flash of '28 and UK All-America, peeled off his sports coat, undid his tie and ran to the scorer's table, where he pounded his fist and announced, "Coach Johnson in for Morehead!" Recountings that value color over truth had Johnson dashing up and down the court with the players the last minute and 40 seconds. The next year, on arrival at Tennessee Tech, Johnson used the arena microphone to ask all spectators to "please synchronize your watches." That was Johnson's last year in the OVC.

On a foundation laid by Ellis Johnson in a 15-year coaching job (176 victories, 158 losses), Morehead State came to rank second to Western Kentucky in number of OVC championships won or shared. Bobby Laughlin's teams won four championships in 12 seasons, Bob Wright added one and Bill Harrell won two before getting into trouble with Adron Doran. With some important OVC games coming up, Harrell left his top six players at home when Morehead went to Illinois State for a non-conference game. Illinois State cried fraud, embarrassed Morehead nationally — the affair was entitled "The Missing Six" — and Doran didn't resist when Harrell said he would resign. Morehead shared the league championship that year. Crazy league.

One time the OVC combatants called cease-fire. In March of 1971, Western Kentucky played the University of Kentucky in the NCAA Mideast Regional. The teams had never before met, a circumstance explained by UK's arrogance in dealing with the state's other universities. "It was like the Chinese, Americans

Cal Luther of Murray State, 1969.

and Russians having a love-in," Cal Luther said of the OVC's unity in support of Western. "It was remarkable, really. I found myself rooting for those gawddamn red uniforms for the first time in my life. Of course, it didn't take me long to get over that insanity and I'm back to hating them again." Western left Kentucky in a daze, a 107-83 loser, and went on to finish third in the NCAA Tournament — only to be forced to return the trophy two years later when All-America Jim McDaniels was shown to have signed a pro contract early in his senior year. Crazy league.

For whatever respect the Ohio Valley Conference had across the nation, it needed thank Western Kentucky and Ed Diddle. Not to mention the coach's red towel. With that string of 20-victory seasons that began in 1934, Western established its basketball reputation at a regional level. The step up to the Big Time came in 1941. A persistent selling job by Kelly Thompson, then the school's publicity man, convinced Ned Irish, the boss at Madison Square Garden, that Ed Diddle, The Man With the Red Towel, was a show in himself and with a good team would add fun to the National Invitation Tournament. "Ned Irish asked me to throw that towel wide and high — and I did," Diddle said. Western finished second in the 1941 NIT.

Diddle first sent the towel flying, he said, in a game against Tennessee Tech. "We were one point behind. Carl Lamar had the ball, and I screamed at him to shoot. He squatted down and put reverse English on the ball.

"Well, it went in, and when it did, I threw my towel 'way up in the air. It was hot in that barn and I'd been wiping my hands and face all night. The towel was wet as water. It came down on my head. I looked like an Indian squaw with that towel over my head.

"So the boys said, 'Coach, we can't win unless you throw that towel up.' And along came radio, TV, public relations men and high-powered newspapermen writing about it. So I kept it up."

Diddle's repertoire of towel tricks was impressive. He threw the towel to the rafters, beat it against the floor, cried into it, stuffed it into his mouth. It soon became a symbol of his emotions, visible to all, and as such it was outlawed by the rulemakers who thought towel-waving might incite crowds against referees. George Barker of the Nashville Tennessean provided an interpretation of Diddle's antics with his towel:

"Tossed high into the air: Pure climactic joy.

"Whirled overhead: Satisfaction and gay expectations.

"Slapped violently on the floor: Extreme disappointment with players or referees.

"Twisted or braided: Outcome doubtful.

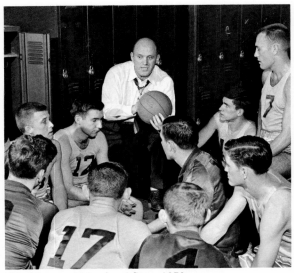

Ellis Johnson of Morehead State, 1953.

"Chewed: Outcome very doubtful.

"Used to shield eyes: Horror, or Shakespearean dismay."

In 1950 Western lost at Murray State. Students began a chant: "We want the towel, we want the towel." Diddle waved to them and walked to the Murray cheerleaders. He put his towel around the neck of one and gave them all a kiss on the cheek. Even in retirement, Diddle came to Western's games — in a 13,500-seat palace called E. A. Diddle Arena, once proclaimed by its namesake as "the best damn E. A. Diddle Arena in America" — and led cheers by waving a red towel. Diddle was 72 when he climbed onto a press table at courtside. Western was losing to Dayton. A Dayton newspaperman said, "Hey, get down from there! You can't stand up there!"

Diddle looked at him. "Son, I own this place," he said. He spun his towel overhead.

Ed Diddle Jr. cried. He stood before his father's casket on Jan. 4, 1970. A bear of a man, tall and thick, he played basketball for his dad in the late '40s. When Ed Jr. became a college coach, too, going to

127

Jim McDaniels and coach Johnny Oldham of Western Kentucky. McDaniels had just scored 46 points in a 1970 victory over Artis Gilmore and Jacksonville University in Freedom Hall. McDaniels grew up in Scottsville, only 25 miles from Bowling Green. "I drove to Scottsville to see Mac so often I could've done it blindfolded," Oldham said.

Some 1-on-3 basketball, McDaniels style. With five starters from the state, Western Kentucky enjoyed its greatest moment with this 107-83 victory over Kentucky in the 1971 NCAA Mideast Regional at Athens, Ga. UK players from left are Jim Andrews, Larry Steele and Mike Casey. In McDaniels' three seasons, Western won 65 games and lost 19, won two OVC championships and won the third-place game in the 1971 NCAA Tournament.

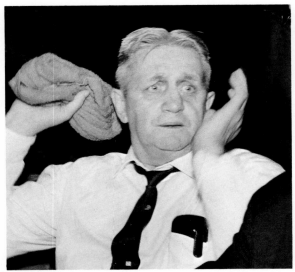
Diddle, his towel and frustration.

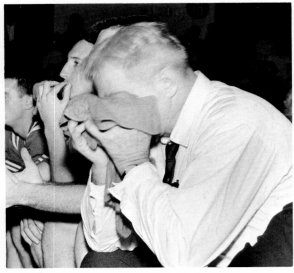
Anguish.

Middle Tennessee, he first took his team against his dad's boys on Jan. 31, 1957.

Western won the game, 79-72, but it wasn't easy. And Ed Diddle Sr., then 61 years old, breathed a sigh of relief when victory was accomplished.

"You know," he said, talking about his son, "that little scare had me scamped for a while."

The scamp stood before his father's casket and cried. The old coach had on a red-and-white striped tie. A red handkerchief was in his breast pocket. The coach had in his folded hands a red towel, this one with black script lettering that read, "Coach Diddle."

Softly, his voice cracking, Ed Diddle Jr. said, "He was a good one."

Ed Diddle leaving "the best damn E. A. Diddle Arena."

"LOUISVILLE'S EATING T-BONE STEAKS. THEY'RE WINNERS."

In 1944 Adolph Rupp was inducted into the Helms Athletic Foundation Hall of Fame for his contributions to college basketball. Ed Diddle's teams, in 1944, had won 20 games a year for 10 straight seasons. In Louisville that year, a high school coach named Bernard (Peck) Hickman, once a star player for Diddle, quit at Valley High, where he was adored, to take what he called "the worst job in America." The evidence suggests Hickman spoke too kindly of the basketball program at the University of Louisville.

The Louisville teams won a total of 29 games the six years before Hickman arrived. In 1939 and '40, Louisville won a single game each season. It lost 33 times (twice to something or someone called Alfred Holbrook). Belknap Gym was Louisville's home court, a basketball house distinguished by bleachers on one side only. Overcome by a mad desire to see Louisville play Alfred Holbrook, about 500 customers could squeeze into Belknap. That never happened. The most money Louisville ever took in at the gate was $210.

At Valley High, Hickman took his team to the hallowed state tournament three times in five years. Every Christmas he was given a gift of $300 to $500 by a Santa Claus-ish fan who would stuff the money into Hickman's pocket. Another basketball addict provided Hickman a house rent-free.

For coaching, doing the laundry and marking lines on the Belknap Gym floor, Louisville paid Hickman $2,400. That was $600 less than he made at Valley. The university's basketball budget was $300. Trying to explain the foolishness that led him to leave Valley for Louisville, Hickman 30 years later said, "Anything I did at Louisville — if I won one ball game — would be better than they were used to." He was 32 years old and ambitious. Whatever Louisville basketball would become, whether it remained bush league or moved to the bigs, Peck Hickman would be the man responsible.

March 17, 1961. Louisville against Ohio State, the defending national champion, winner of 29 straight games. First game of the NCAA Mideast Regional. In Freedom Hall, with 18,833 spectators on hand.

In 1948 Louisville won the National Association of Intercollegiate Basketball

Peck Hickman, 1967.

championship, a small-college affair. In '56 Louisville won the NIT. "My goals were very simple," Peck Hickman said later. "I wanted to win what I called the 'Triple Crown'—the NAIB, the NIT and the NCAA. I'd be the only coach who ever won all three."

So in March of 1961, Hickman dearly wanted a victory over an Ohio State team whose best players were Jerry Lucas and John Havlicek.

"Yeah, that doggone Havlicek," Hickman said nearly a decade and a half later. "We might have made it if it hadn't been for him.

"That was my greatest disappointment. We had Ohio State down by five points with just a couple minutes to go. Then I outcoached myself."

Desperate in those last two minutes, Ohio State turned to a pressing defense. A Louisville guard, a sophomore named Jadie Frazier, violated a Hickman rule— "Never take the ball to the sidelines against the trap"— and lost the ball twice to the Ohioans.

"I turned to John (Dromo, his assistant coach) and said, 'You think the pressure's getting to Jadie?' Then we sent in Ron Rubenstein. He was a senior."

Rubenstein promptly committed the same sins. "He took the ball into the corner twice and lost it both times," Hickman said. It was inexplicable. "He'd been here four years, and he knew the rule."

Louisville built its lead with the help of a jury-rigged defense designed to render Jerry Lucas inoperative. "We knew Ohio State didn't play very well unless Lucas got the ball," Hickman said. All night long at least three Louisville defenders were within an arm's reach of the All-America center. Lucas took only seven shots, making two, and scored nine points, barely a third of his average. "And I told our center, Fred Sawyer, that I didn't care if he only got one rebound —just block Lucas off the boards." Though Lucas had 18 rebounds to Sawyer's seven, Ohio State beat Louisville only 42-41 on the boards, a far cry from the champions' usual rebounding domination.

The Louisvilles were physical, which in basketball talk means they shoved people around a lot. They had the nation's tallest front line: Sawyer, 6 feet 11; Bud Olsen, 6-8; and John Turner, 6-5. The

John Havlicek's jumper put Ohio State ahead 56-54.

primary guards were Howard Stacey, Frazier and Rubenstein. Winners of their first 13 games in that season, Hickman's charges lost four of their last six regular-season games. "We just had a letdown," the coach said. Against Ohio State, Louisville was a composed band of battlers. The game was tied at 54-all with 40 seconds to play.

Turner, an All-America, then bounced the ball off his foot and out of bounds. Ohio State missed a shot with 29 seconds to play, but a reserve forward named Bobby Knight grabbed the re-

bound, giving the Buckeyes another chance. With six seconds to go, from 20 feet out on the right side, John Havlicek threw in a jump shot. Ohio State led 56-54.

Then, driving, Turner was fouled when Siegfried fell in front of him. He would shoot the one-and-one. There was one second left in the game. By then Turner had 24 points and 15 rebounds. He made the first free throw. The second bounced around the rim before falling off to one side. The ball was tipped back to Turner and he missed a 15-footer at game's end. "I really felt that was the year we could take all the marbles," Hickman said.

The next night Ohio State beat Kentucky 87-74. It lost in the NCAA championship game to Cincinnati. Louisville ended that season with a 21-8 record, and though Hickman twice more reached the NCAA regionals he would never be closer to his Triple Crown. Hickman never named the best of his 23 Louisville teams, but certainly the choice would come to that 1961 outfit or the 1956 team that won the NIT.

"The NIT team had more confidence in themselves than any I ever had," Hickman said. "I never saw a team with more heart. They were determined to win, confident they would win — and they did."

The star was Charlie Tyra, 6-8 and brute strong. He averaged 23.8 points and 22.2 rebounds a game. "He wasn't quick, but he was quick enough," Hickman said. "He had a decent hook shot. He was just real, real strong and aggressive. He was a tremendous rebounder." He was an All-America that season, his junior year. The forwards were Bill Dar-

John Turner of Louisville (22) is fouled by Larry Siegfried (21).

Turner made one free throw, but missed the second.

Louisville's cheerleaders weep after the 56-55 defeat.

ragh and Herb Harrah. The three top guards were Phil Rollins, Jim Morgan and Gerry Moorman. Louisville won 26 of 29 games, and won the NIT with three easy victories, none by less than 10 points. Tyra was the tournament's Most Valuable Player.

By then, however, the NIT was no longer *the* tournament. Once strictly an invitational, the NCAA prospered when it changed its tournament format to admit automatically certain conference champions. Too, the NCAA expanded the number of entrants, making it truly repre-

sentative of all regions of the country. And the NIT, already laboring under the heavy burden of the point-shaving scandals that seemed to breed in New York, lost its position of eminence. After Ralph Beard, Alex Groza and Dale Barnstable admitted taking gamblers' money, Kentucky never again played in the original Madison Square Garden — where in 1946 a gum-chomping, 18-year-old, scared-to-death Beard made a free throw to win the NIT.

If Louisville wanted credibility, it needed more than a victory in a tourna-

This wild bunch won the 1956 NIT for Louisville.

ment of declining prestige. Especially was that the case in the city of Louisville and in Kentucky, where the basketball patrons were accustomed to UK's habit of NCAA championships. Louisville needed to beat UK. Only that way could anyone believe Louisville was first-class. Problem was, the teams never played each other.

It was Kentucky's desire to play no other university in the state. The reasoning was plain. UK had nothing to gain. At Western Kentucky, Ed Diddle never proposed a Western-UK game. "He thought both schools were doing right well in their own bailiwicks," said Kelly Thompson, the coach's long-time confidante. "Of course, if a situation had developed that brought the teams together, it would not have displeased Mr. Diddle." Thompson described Diddle and Rupp as "aloofly friendly, with great respect for each other, but I don't believe you could call them buddies." For his part, Hickman never tried to schedule Kentucky. The schools met only in post-season tournaments. They first played in the 1948 Olympic trials when Louisville, the NAIB representative, lost to UK's NCAA champions 91-57. The next two meetings came in the NCAA Tournament. In 1951 UK won 79-68. And then in 1959 Louisville, in its 15th season under Hickman, beat the defending national champions 76-61 in the Midwest Regional at Evanston, Ill. It was only the third loss in 26 games for a UK team led by All-America Johnny Cox and Bill Lickert.

"Our boys were scared going into that game," Hickman said. "They were too cautious, afraid to let their hair down. Kentucky got us down nine or 11 points and was putting pressure on us defensively.

"I called timeout and said I didn't

John Turner beats UK's Don Mills to the ball in 1959.

want to see any daylight between us and their guards. I wanted to put the pressure right back on them. And at halftime, I decided to press all over the floor all the time."

At game's end, Rupp walked to Hickman and said, "By gawd, you laid the wood to us tonight." Hickman added a postscript. "I don't know if it's true, but one of my players told me that Adolph was really raking his kids up one side and down the other after the game. He said Adolph told them, 'You know what Louisville's eating tonight? T-bone steaks.

136

They're winners. You guys get a dollar to eat hamburgers.'"

That Louisville team had Harold Andrews and Roger Tieman at guard, Fred Sawyer at center, John Turner and Don Goldstein at forwards. Another victory at Evanston put Louisville in the NCAA semifinals on its home court, Freedom Hall. There Louisville lost to West Virginia, which in turn lost the national championship game to California. For Louisville, only once before a contestant in the NCAA Tournament, 1959 was a very good year. "Beating Kentucky," Hickman said, "was a case of us finally establishing ourselves as a national power — the final step."

The first steps, if we trace them to their beginnings, came in Central City, Ky., where the Golden Tide basketball team was big stuff. "They had a great basketball tradition," Hickman said of his hometown. "If you were a boy who could walk, you played basketball. If you didn't, there weren't a lot of people who would associate with you."

One of five sons of railroader George Rollin Henry Harry Hickman ("They named him after all his uncles to keep peace in the family. He was called Rolly."), the future coach grew up playing basketball and baseball. He also boxed. "Anytime anybody came looking for me, my mother said, 'He's down at the ball park with the other bums.'"

After Hickman made the All-Tournament team in the 1929 State Tournament, in which Central City lost to eventual winner Heath, he had a choice to make.

"I could have played pro baseball," he said. "But my dad said no. He had five kids and none ever went to college. He said I was going to college."

Hickman is happy after beating Kentucky 76-61.

Or Hickman might have been a professional boxer.

"I was pretty fair. Over at Drakesboro one time, I fought in the recreation hall where they had boxing, wrestling, roller skating. A big guy with a cigar set it up for me to fight my brother, Paul. Said we'd get $50 each plus expenses.

"When the fight was over, I went to get my money. The big, ol' fat guy had his feet up on the desk. Had a cigar, smoking it. And he said he wasn't going to pay me. He said it might be against school rules and then I couldn't play basketball

137

and Central City would kill him. Well, $50 back then was like $5,000 in 1975. So I said, 'You mean you're not going to pay me anything?'

"He said, 'Here's $5, kid, to pay your gas.' I told him what he could do with it.

"Later, some guy out of Chicago came to Central City. He wanted to take me out boxing. My dad was on a rocking chair on the front porch. Every time the guy would say something, my dad would say, 'He's going to college,' It didn't make any difference if the guy had said it was raining. My dad would keep rocking and say, 'He's going to college.'"

Because Central City is only about 65 miles from Bowling Green, Hickman naturally fell under the spell of Ed Diddle. He was a four-year regular at Western Kentucky from 1931 to 1935. "Peck played with that head of his," Diddle once said. "He was very smart. You only had to tell him something once and he had it. I never had any trouble with him, either. Only thing, all the girls liked him. That was the hardest part I had with him. But Peck loved to play and he only went out when the season was over."

Hickman didn't plan to coach. He was a pre-med student with designs on being a surgeon. "But the Depression came along the first half of my junior year and I couldn't afford the instruments in pre-med." His first coaching job was at Hodgenville High School, where the All-Stater from Central City, Mr. Big Shot from Western Kentucky, learned a lesson he never forgot.

"I thought I knew pretty much," Hickman said later. He had bushy eyebrows above deepset eyes in a bulldog's face. In moments of self-deprecation, Hickman caused the right eyebrow to rise while he seemed to grind his teeth behind

Peck Hickman, a dashing guard, 1931.

a smile. "I told those boys if their man blinked his left eye, they should blink their right. I told them where to shoot, how to play defense — what to do every minute. I had them so overcoached they didn't know what to do.

"We finished with three wins and 18 losses, the only losing season I've ever had. I probably did more 'coaching' that year than in any since."

In March of that season, Hickman caught a ride to the State Tournament with another high school basketball coach, Frank Camp, then at Glasgow. Hickman was awash in a sea of self-pity. "I can't coach, I'm going to quit," he announced to Camp. "My team was three and 18."

Camp said, "You've had a *good* season. I lost 22 straight."

"Stop the car! Stop the car!" Hickman said. He pulled out a pencil and a little black book. "Just when can we get together for a couple games next season?"

The travail even affected Hickman's social life. "We courted for five years, but Peck stayed so mad we didn't get married," the coach's wife said. "Peck hated to lose and his teams were losing. I think Peck decided he was going to be a winner when he won a marble-shooting contest in Central City. He was just a little boy then. He's still got the cup they gave him."

From Hodgenville to Valley to Louisville, his ill-treated sweetheart in tow, Hickman moved quickly and with purpose. A war was on when he arrived at Belknap Gym. "The basketball players were all there on a V-12 program. The Navy. A lieutenant came in the first day of practice and said, 'You men are needed across the pond. So if coach Hickman has any troubles with you, you'll be gone the next morning.'

"Hell, I could've told them to run into a brick wall and they'd have said, 'How hard?' I had no discipline problems." Besides that, they were fair basketball players and Hickman's first Louisville team had a 16-3 record. Over the next six years, playing an increasingly difficult schedule ("We couldn't build a reputation on a pitty-pat schedule"), Louisville averaged 22 victories a season.

"With the Navy players, we knocked off some teams we probably shouldn't have," Hickman said. "That started some interest among Louisville alumni and when the Navy program was abandoned we had scholarships to give away for the first time in the school's history. We got better players, and so we had better teams.

"Then we hit it lucky. We won the NAIB. That team included Jack Coleman, Johnny Knopf, Kenny Reeves, Dee Compton, Button Combs, Ish Combs and Oz Johnson. When we got back from the tournament in Kansas City, 7,500 people were at the train station.

"When you win, it creates a lot of enthusiasm. We were on our way."

To where? The NIT. "We hadn't been able to get a foot in the door," Hickman said. "Then I invited Ned Irish down to speak at our basketball banquet." Irish was the boss of Madison Square Garden, the NIT promoter. Hickman smiled at the fond remembrance. "He stood up there and read statistics about Madison Square Garden. He was awful." A look of full contentment settled on Hickman's face. "He was awful, but we were invited to the NIT the next year."

That was 1952. Louisville played in the tournament every season until it won

John Dromo's teams were 80-31 in four seasons.

it in '56. Hickman retired as coach after the 1966-67 season in which Louisville, led by All-America Westley Unseld, won 23 games, lost five and was ranked No. 2 to UCLA and Lew Alcindor most of the year. "My last season the basketball program brought in $400,000," said the coach whose first gym had seats on one side only.

Hickman's successor was John Dromo, his long-time assistant coach who had done the outstanding recruiting that kept Louisville well-stocked with good players. In Hickman's last season, Louisville won 20 games for the first time since it lost to Ohio State five years before. Under Dromo, Louisville went 21-7, 21-6, 18-9 and 20-9. It appeared in the NCAA once, the NIT three times.

When it came time, in the spring of 1971, to hire a new coach to take over from Dromo, who had suffered a heart attack, an assistant coach at UCLA said he would be interested. "Louisville is one of the best jobs in the country," said Denny Crum.

THE NEW KEEPERS OF TRADITION

To understand how Denny Crum came to be known to many people as Denny the Crumb, we need remember that Ed Diddle never questioned the supremacy of the University of Kentucky basketball program. Nor did Peck Hickman. As Kentuckians accepted the air they breathed, so did they accept UK's divinity. It was a gift from on high, and they paused in their daily labors to bow toward Lexington, where kindly old Adolph worked his miracles. And then from Southern California, from Lotus Land, from 2,000 miles away, from the cursed UCLA team that had just won its sixth NCAA championship, leaving Kentucky's four titles in the dust — from *out there somewhere* came Denny Crum. He came to the University of *Louisville*. His luggage included no diplomacy.

If a newspaperman asked a question of Crum, Crum answered it. So in January of 1972, in the first month of Crum's first season, someone asked the coach what he thought of the freshmen playing at UK. Around the state, the natives regarded those freshmen as godlings.

"I was not overly impressed with any of them," Crum said.

The newspaperman backed away a bit, lest he too be struck by the lightning sure to zap such an infidel. But none came, and Crum went on talking. He had a freshman at Louisville named Allen Murphy who "would eat any of UK's guys alive." The best of UK's group was Kevin Grevey, Crum said, because he'd played in metropolitan competition, unlike Mike Flynn and Jimmy Dan Conner.

Would Crum compare Kentucky's freshmen with those he had recruited the previous spring at UCLA?

"UK's wouldn't compare," Crum said.

The natives, restless by now, wrote unfriendly letters, one addressed to "Denny Crumb," another to the "Louisville Crum and Bugle Corps." Crum said he answered every one. "I was pleased they were reading about us," he said.

It was Adolph Rupp who once said, "Anything for a column." It was Rupp who popped off in all directions, Rupp the Irreverent. If Denny Crum forgot to pack diplomacy, he carried from California his considerable ego, just as Rupp had done on the train from Freeport to Lexington. Funny, the way things work. What Kentuckians adored in Adolph, they abhorred in Crum, because, of course, they could see signs of greatness in Crum's work — and that work was done at *Louisville*, by gawd. In most states, *the* big city is the source of distrust in rural areas. That natural suspicion, born of our fears of the unknown, was greatly multiplied in Kentucky, where Louisville, with a metropolitan population of nearly 800,000, was the state's only city with over 175,000 people. Kentuckians didn't want to hear a *Louisville* coach say anything but good-bye.

Rupp wore brown suits to the bench. Joe B. Hall, the Baron's successor, favored businessman blue. One-on-one with Crum, a rainbow had no chance. Tall and trim, his hair carefully cut and purposefully styled (the purpose being to cover balding areas), Crum worked in greens and reds and yellows, plaids and stripes, suits and Levis. Rupp was a dictator who brooked no sass. Riled once by a player who talked back to him on the bench, Rupp ordered the equipment manager to clean out the offender's locker. He was off the team. The player found out the next day when he asked where his gear was. Bernie Shively, the UK athletic director, was shaken when a reporter relayed the player's version of the incident. "Nobody ever asked the player's side before," Shively said. At Louisville, Crum came to work in new togs and he brought new ideas.

"On our squad, we only have two rules: You have to go to class and you've got to be on time. We don't have a curfew. We don't have any rules about drinking and smoking...We police each other," he said.

"I'm fair with them, that's the secret. I don't treat them all equally because you can't — they're not all equal. They get what they earn. I'm not gonna upset my star player by sitting him on the bench.

"I treat them as adults. I don't expect them to do anything I wouldn't. Hell, I go out at night and have a drink and horse around. They'd be looking for a new coach around here if I suspended a guy because he had a beer. Let's be realistic. Times have changed."

Crum was an absolute competitor. No game was designed to kill time. Once, a man who had never played gin rummy sat down to the card table with Crum (whose in-game conversation is so incessantly annoying that John Wooden told him, "Denny, you're the world's greatest card player...from nose to chin.") The novice pleaded for mercy from Crum. Three minutes later, the novice owed Crum $7.48. "I play to win," the coach said sharply.

He missed few tricks during a basketball game, either. It was said Wooden built his empire on organization, that during a game he was reluctant to make "moves," a coach's word for tactical changes and adjustments. Wooden, like Rupp, believed his superior forces, executing their basic plays, would prevail in the end, so why tinker? Crum confessed his infatuation with strategy and tactics. One example suffices: In a big game at Tulsa, Crum's center, Wesley Cox, was tumbled to the floor on a foul.

Even before the referees asked Cox if he were hurt, Crum had a substitute off the bench and into the game. How did Crum know Cox was hurt badly enough to be taken out?

"Cox was shooting 65 per cent on free throws, and the guy I sent in for him was shooting about 80 per cent," the coach said, smiling.

When the substitute made the free

throw, Cox immediately came back into the game for him. A miracle recovery.

On arrival in Louisville in 1971, Crum was 34 years old. He'd been a playmaking guard for Wooden and coached the UCLA freshmen two years before working at Pierce Junior College six seasons. He returned to UCLA as Wooden's No. 1 assistant in 1968 and was there for the middle three of UCLA's seven straight NCAA championships. The Louisville job, though full of promise, was a minefield for a bright young coach.

Crum's predecessor, John Dromo,

Denny Crum of Louisville (left) meets his old boss, Johnny Wooden of UCLA, before their teams played in the 1975 NCAA Tournament semifinals.

had resigned because of heart trouble. Cynics said the heart trouble was produced by a bunch of talented, undisciplined players who had potential without desire. For two years under Dromo, those players failed in the important games.

They would be seniors for Crum. A new coach. Old players. Big things expected. Would it work? One of those seniors was Jim Price, a guard who under Dromo had been a showboat only. For Crum, he was a leader — an All-America who would be a No. 1 draft pick by the pros. By season's end that first year, the

Louisville's Phillip Bond passes around Richard Washington.

Bond comes upcourt against Washington.

Washington (31) puts UCLA ahead with two seconds to play.

In orbit. Junior Bridgeman of Louisville scores against UCLA.
far left.

Dig the threads.

new coach had reshaped the old players. Louisville made it to the Final Four of the NCAA Tournament, there to lose — funny, the way things work out — to UCLA. The record: 26-5.

Crum's task the next season was the reverse. Now he had to win with young, inexperienced players, the likes of Allen Murphy and Junior Bridgeman. None of Crum's starters had ever started a college game. They won 23 games, lost seven. And if these first two seasons established Crum as a coach of promise, the next two years certified his ability beyond doubt.

With a 6-foot-5 freshman center, Louisville was 21-7 and won the Missouri Valley Conference championship in 1974. Before the 1974-75 season, someone asked Crum if Louisville could win the national championship. "Yes, sir," Crum said. Not many coaches seek out the burden of great expectations. But if you ask Crum a question, you get an answer. "I'm not a pop-off," he said, "I'm just honest." As it happened, Louisville again won the championship of one of America's best conferences, for the third time in Crum's first four years, and it advanced

for the second time to the Final Four of the NCAA, there to lose — funny — to UCLA by one point in an overtime period. Only a missed free throw by a Louisville senior who had not missed a single free throw all *season* allowed UCLA to escape defeat in regulation time. "We were the better team," Crum said. "If we played UCLA 10 times, we'd win eight of them — or maybe nine." The record that year was 28-3. For four years, Crum's record was 98-22. Those were numbers Rupp could appreciate.

If not for that missed free throw, the proud basketball families of Louisville and UK, the new keepers of tradition that began in Halstead and Central City, would have played for the national championship in San Diego in late March of 1975. Ah, so sweet the dream, so sorrowful the awakening. For Joe B. Hall, the trip to San Diego was his first appearance in the Final Four. A victory over Syracuse in the semifinals put UK against UCLA for the big prize. It was a match ordained by history. Kentucky, once the king unchallenged. UCLA, a dynasty in full bloom. Between them, they owned 13 of the 36 NCAA championships, all won in the last 27 years.

Denny Crum spoke in the pre-season of great expectations. Joe Hall didn't say much, and much of what he said was discounted, for in his first two seasons the natives decided that this was not Adolph Rupp reborn, this was a pretender to the throne. George Selkirk followed Babe Ruth in right field for the Yankees. Whatever happened to George Selkirk? "I'd like to succeed the man who succeeds Rupp," said Ralph Carlisle in prediction that the poor fellow would inevitably fail. Rupp did nothing to make Hall's ascension painless. He fought retirement. After

Joe Hall and his boss, The Baron, 1972.

a fitful start, Hall's first team finally won 10 straight games before losing in the final of the Mideast Regional. Its record was 20-8. "A disappointing season," Rupp said on a television show he did even in retirement.

The next year, with Kevin Grevey and Mike Flynn and Jimmy Dan Conner juniors, UK was 13-13, and people made up small poems that went, "Joe must go. . . . Hall must fall." Through it all, the man who had hired Hall as an assistant, the man who begged him to return when he had already left UK and accepted the head coaching job at St. Louis (Hall jilted St. Louis after five days, returning to UK with Rupp's promise he would help make Hall his successor) — through Hall's 13-13 travail, Rupp was mute, and his silence was taken as criticism.

"This job, more than any other in the country, is made harder by the reflections back to the Rupp years, by Rupp's presence here, by his contact with the players," Hall said in the middle of that long season. "But I'm not alibiing, I'm just trying to explain why I've had trouble selling my program so far. The problems I'm having are going to be solved — and I'll solve them myself."

In Hall's third season, one that would find UK again in a game for the national championship, the coach and his players produced a series of dramas remarkable for their intensity. This was basketball soap-opera style. The first scene showed UK running wild in a 97-70 victory over Northwestern, after which guard Mike Flynn said of UK's aggressive defense, "That's the way you have to play to win the NCAA." Flynn smiled nervously at the audacity of his words. A 13-13 team talking about winning the NCAA? Whoa, Mike. "Well, that's what everyone dreams about," Flynn said, shrugging his shoulders.

In the third game of the season, Indiana University beat Kentucky 98-74 at Bloomington. It wasn't that close. Only the mercy of IU coach Bob Knight kept the margin of victory under 50 points. Grevey, on the team bus to Lexington that night, sat alone in the dark. He thought, "What's wrong with us?" He had, he said later, "second doubts about us."

Defeat was not Kentucky's only injury that day. Late in the game, during a mild debate on the sidelines, Knight concluded the talk by cuffing Hall sharply across the back of the head. Knight later said it was a friendly gesture, with no harm meant, but Hall took offense. With 17,700 people to see it, he had been treated condescendingly by his opposite number. He would not soon forget. Doomsayers sent up moans. Here we go again. All the signs of the previous year's disaster were there. UK was uptight. No confidence. No grace under pressure. When does football season start?

Then, two days later, came North Carolina. Ranked in the top 10, fresh

Hall was angry when Bob Knight of IU slapped his head.

from an impressive road victory at Houston, Carolina figured to beat UK badly, even in Freedom Hall. A local bookmaker said $8,700 was bet on Carolina, $200 on UK. With Conner scoring 35 points, Kentucky rolled from an early 22-8 deficit to win 90-78. Amazing.

UK followed with four more victories in three weeks, including the demolition of Kansas and Notre Dame, considered fine teams. "We're real this year," said Jimmy Dan Conner, the team's spiritual leader. The transformation was complete. Dr. Jekyll doing his Mr. Hyde bit was small potatoes next to Kentucky's act. The year before, Kentucky was not a basketball team. It was a nervous breakdown in sneakers. You didn't watch games, you sat in on group therapy.

Came March 22, 1975. In the championship game of the NCAA Mideast Regional, Kentucky played Indiana. A hyperbolic sports writer (blush) later called it the greatest college game ever played. Here's what he wrote that day. . . .

DAYTON, Ohio — A woman with a big smile and dancing eyes tapped Joe Hall on the shoulder. The University of Kentucky basketball coach was talking

to reporters. "Can I interrupt the coach?" said Katharine Hall, who as the coach's wife knew the answer to that one.

Hall put his right arm around her, pulling her close to him, and they kissed on the basketball court at the University of Dayton Arena. Only minutes earlier, Kentucky had beaten Indiana 92-90 in a game full of cardiac arrests.

"Great, just *great*," Hall said into his wife's ear.

If Kentucky ever, in its rich history, played a more important game with more ferocity, someone will have to prove it to the 13,458 folks here.

By winning, UK is the NCAA's Mideast Regional champion and advances to the Final Four next Saturday in San Diego. It will play Syracuse, champion of the East Regional.

By winning, UK ended Indiana's 34-game winning streak, handing the No. 1-ranked Hoosiers their first defeat of a remarkable season, in which they performed with such precision that they dispatched opponents by an average of 23 points a game.

By winning, UK ended a melancholy streak of failure in the regional finals.

148

Since Kentucky finished second in the 1966 NCAA Tournament, it had lost four times in the regional championship game.

UK did it with straight basketball. No tricks. No holding the ball. Lesser teams might have tried something crazy — especially a team that had lost to Indiana 98-74 on Dec. 7, as UK had. Somebody asked Jimmy Dan Conner, a UK guard, if his team came into yesterday's game with trepidation.

"No," Conner said. "When we went out of the locker room to play, we were *angry*. They beat us so bad the time before. We wanted to get 'em."

UK won because its guards, Conner and Mike Flynn, scored 39 points — 18 over their combined average. And it won because its defense, aggressive and enthusiastic, broke Indiana's poise. Normally efficient and careful, Indiana was forced into 20 turnovers yesterday.

"They got that look on their faces that a coach likes to see in the opponents," Hall said.

What look?

"Like a look of wonder at what's happening."

It was, in fact, a wonder. People who make their living betting on sports events figured Indiana to win by 12 points. A Louisville sports editor (guess who) said Indiana would win 93-81. He said UK could win only if Kevin Grevey, the star forward, scored 25 or 30 points. He said Indiana's Quinn Buckner would control Mike Flynn.

Wrong, wrong, wrong.

Flynn scored 22 points, nearly triple his average. He made six of six shots in the decisive second half. At game's end, they raised Flynn up last to give him the honor of cutting the final strand that held the net to the rim. Taking it in hand, Flynn

shook it in the direction of the Indiana rooters.

"I was thinking about all the times Indiana had beaten us, and all that stuff I've had to take back home," he said.

Flynn grew up in Jeffersonville. He was Indiana's "Mr. Basketball" in 1971. When he chose to play at Kentucky, and when Indiana beat Flynn and UK four straight times, the noise in Jeff grew.

"They'd say, 'I told you, you should have gone to IU. They're winning. They're better than Kentucky.'

"And Indiana proved it. So what could I say? They had me."

Flynn sat at courtside, the net a necklace. He smiled. "Now maybe I can do some talking."

For Flynn, for Grevey, for Conner and Bob Guyette — UK's senior starters — yesterday's victory was redemption.

"I came to Kentucky to win a national championship and be All-America," Flynn said. "I won't be an All-America, but we still have a shot at the national championship."

Joe Hall recruited these seniors. While assistant to Adolph Rupp, Hall coached them as freshmen. He became boss the next year, and the four seasons have been full of drama.

"My freshman year we were 22-0 and ranked No. 1 in the country," Flynn said. "We couldn't have asked for anything better.

"As sophomores, we started out slow. A lot of things were going wrong. We'd had a lot of publicity, and there was a lot of pressure — and we weren't ready for it."

UK won 10 games in a row that year before losing to — yes — Indiana in the Mideast Regional championship game. The UK record was 20-8. Not bad most

Mike Flynn of Kentucky works past Indiana's Kent Benson in NCAA. *far left.*

UK's Kevin Grevey turns his back on Indiana's Bobby Wilkerson. *left.*

Kentucky's six seniors enjoyed the 92-90 victory over Indiana in the 1975 Mideast Regional. From left are G. J. Smith, Jerry Hale, Jimmy Dan Conner (mostly hidden), Bob Guyette, Kevin Grevey and Mike Flynn. *below.*

places, but at a school that has won four national championships, 20 victories is mediocre.

If 20-8 is mediocre, what is 13-13? "The downfall of our career," Flynn said of the 1973-74 season. "We let a lot of people down, and they started saying we weren't as good as we were supposed to be. We didn't live up to their expectations."

The problem, Flynn said, was one of manpower. "We just didn't have the big man. We had a small guard, two small forwards and no big man. That's changed now."

Any explanation of UK's turnaround — from 13-13 to 25-4 with two more victories needed for a national championship — must begin with UK's two 6-foot-10 freshman centers, Rick Robey and Mike Phillips.

Because they contributed so significantly and so quickly, Hall could use the 6-9 Guyette at forward and the 6-4 Conner at guard. Suddenly, a small UK team was a very large team.

Robey brought more than size. He is a fighter, and his aggressiveness rubbed off. If UK is anything, it is, to use a coaching word, "physical." That means it hits lots of people with lots of shoulders, elbows and hips. Somebody asked Conner how UK handled Indiana's screening offense so well.

"Coach Hall decided that any illegal pick would be met with force," Conner said.

The game at times was a heavyweight fight. Twice, fists flew. Guyette decked Kent Benson, IU's 6-11 brute, with a forearm. Benson threw an elbow at Robey, connecting solidly — and it was at that moment, with 5 minutes and 32 seconds to play, that UK's season came full circle.

On Dec. 7, when IU destroyed UK, Benson, a skilled and seasoned sophomore, humiliated Robey, a freshman playing only his third college game. The humiliation included a forearm smash to Robey's teeth. No foul was called.

Did that bother Robey? Was he frightened? Did he want to go home?

"I learned something today," Robey said. He smiled. He was at ease. No big deal. "I'll put it to use."

So yesterday Robey scored 10 points (and Phillips had 10, too). Robey's last two points came on free throws — because this time Benson was caught in the act of delivering the illegal blow. Robey's free throws gave UK a 79-70 lead, its biggest of the game until then.

UK held on to win. "It was 40 minutes of the most intense basketball I've ever seen," Conner said. It would have been easy for a team to fold up after losing to Indiana by 24 in its third game of a season following a 13-13 year. Bob Knight's rap on Hall's head that day could have ruined UK. Hall didn't let it happen. "All I want is another chance to play them," he said in December. "Knight personally humiliated me. I'll never forget it."

From Dec. 7 on, UK grew instead of diminishing, and that was proof of Hall's coaching strength and his team's character. At some point in every game this season, Indiana broke the other guy's will. This time Kentucky refused to be broken. Eyeball to eyeball these teams were, and Indiana blinked. Joe Hall earned Katharine's kiss.

Like Louisville, Kentucky could have beaten UCLA. But like Louisville, Kentucky missed the chance. With six minutes and 23 seconds to play, UCLA led 76-75. Its All-America forward, Dave Meyers, tried an ungainly 20-footer from the top of the key.

After shooting the jump shot, he came down on Kevin Grevey. A foul on Meyers, an official said. Meyers, upset, slapped his palm on the floor and said, "Damn it." That's a technical foul, the official said.

Grevey would get a one-and-one free throw. Also, he'd get to shoot once on the technical. Kentucky could ask for nothing better, because Grevey was an 80 per cent free throw shooter. What's more, UK would keep the ball after the free throw.

It was, then, a possible five-point play if Grevey made all his free throws and UK added a basket afterwards. Kentucky could move from one point behind to four points ahead. The momentum would belong to UK.

Instead, Kentucky got nothing. Zero. Zilch.

Grevey, who scored 34 points, missed both the first of his one-and-one free throws and the technical free throw. And when Kentucky put the ball into play, forward James Lee immediately was called for an offensive foul, giving the ball

back to UCLA. UCLA promptly scored. Instead of being four points behind, UCLA was three points ahead. A seven-point play. Reprieved, UCLA went on to win 92-85.

Denny Crum was *foreign.* Joe Hall was homegrown, the son of Charles Hall, owner of the Cynthiana dry-cleaning plant and twice Harrison County sheriff. He lettered three years in both football and basketball, captained both teams his senior year, was president of his class all four years and had the highest grades of any boy in school. He grew up, one presumes, with an ear pressed against a radio.

"We'd listen to Terry and the Pirates, The Shadow — and Kentucky basketball," he said. "My brother and I would set up coffee cans in bed and throw paper balls into them. We'd play the game right along with the radio."

As a high school player, Hall was good enough to earn a scholarship to UK. He came to school after World War II. "I was the only 'kid' on the squad," Hall said. "Everybody else was coming out of the Army. I was the only guy who didn't

Joe Hall gets a ride after UK's victory over Indiana.

shave." He dearly wanted to play for Rupp. Hall once had a tonsillectomy on a Friday and was back practicing on Wednesday. The result was a hemorrhage that put him in the hospital. That same year, he spent day and night in the hospital with a sprained right ankle and an infected left foot.

"But I'd get out of the hospital long enough each day to go practice," Hall said.

Why?

"Those were the days you didn't miss a practice or you were gone."

The UCLA-Kentucky game for the 1975 national championship was bruising. Richard Washington of UCLA craches into Jimmy Dan Conner en route to a layup. Already on the floor are Rick Robey of Kentucky and Andre McCarter.

U.S. Senator Wendell Ford of Kentucky consoles Bob Guyette after UCLA beat UK 92-85.

It was the Fabulous Five era — "I was the eighth of the Five" — and in two years Hall transferred to the University of the South in Sewanee, Tenn., where he became one of the school's best players ever. He then spent five years in the business world. Among other things, he was a ketchup salesman. At last, Hall pursued his first love, coaching.

His first job was at Shepherdsville in 1956. The second year there, he was his conference's Coach of the Year. He moved to Regis College in Denver, Colo., for a year as an assistant coach and five as the boss. From there he went to Central Missouri State, succeeding Gene Bartow (who would, in time, succeed John Wooden). A year later, Hall returned to Kentucky. It was 1965.

Hall's contributions were immediate and significant. He started a conditioning program that was standard around the country but unknown to Rupp. He did the bulk of UK's recruiting, signing Dan Issel, Mike Pratt, Mike Casey, Tom Parker and all five starters from the 1975 national runnerup team: Flynn, Conner, Guyette, Grevey and Robey. When Harry Lancaster, Rupp's longtime right-hand man, became athletic director in 1969, Hall moved up to be No. 1 assistant.

After the St. Louis affair, and after Rupp decided to give up the fight against retirement, Hall became Kentucky's second coach since Johnny Mauer quit in a huff 43 years earlier. A plain, soft-spoken man most of the time, Hall yet was capable of towering rages. He once engaged a reporter in an hour-long shouting match in a newspaper office. Another time he ordered press-table seating arrangements changed to move certain reporters away from the UK bench. Like Rupp, he chastised players ferociously and sometimes

155

Joe Hall, scrappy guard, 1948. *left.*

Angry at the officials, Joe Hall moved toward them in the 1972 game with North Carolina. Jimmy Dan Conner stops him. *bottom far left.*

The coach at work, 1972.

Was Kentucky excited about beating North Carolina 90-78 in December of 1974? Another silly question. *below*.

considered referees beyond redemption. In one memorable episode, North Carolina led UK by 19 points in Hall's fourth game as coach when this former ketchup salesman made a move.

He ripped off his coat.

He beat it against the floor.

Then he stomped on it.

He tried to get to the referees with his complaint, but Jimmy Dan Conner forcibly restrained him. Kentucky finally lost by only eight points. The tantrum, Hall said, "was the turning point in my life. I had to set fire to the building or something. I made up my mind to get out of coaching if the score continued that way."

At San Diego in March of 1975, someone asked Joe B. Hall what the middle initial stood for.

"Aw, you gotta let me have some mystery about me," the coach said.

Please.

"Bashful," he said.

Come on.

"Basketball," he said with a smile.

Joe Basketball Hall.

Of course.

WHERE HAVE YOU GONE, ORB BOWLING?

The first mascot of the Kentucky Colonels basketball team was a dog. (Considerable testimony says the team was a dog, too, but you know how some people are.) The dog was a Brussels Griffon, a beribboned creature whose proper name was Champion Gaystock LeMonsignor. To his friends, he was Ziggy.

Ziggy had 39 different uniforms, one for each of the Colonels' home games. He also had a tuxedo for moving in the highest circles of dogdom. In those dear, dim, departed days, Ziggy had a seat of his own at courtside. Most often, though, he sat snug in the lap of his mistress, Mamie Gregory, who considered Ziggy an improvement on humans. For the playing of the National Anthem, Ziggy sat at attention. During games Mamie and Ziggy often shared an ice cream cone, taking turns licking it.

Mamie and her husband, Joe, owned the Colonels. The team's logo was a drawing of Ziggy in hot pursuit of a goateed Kentucky Colonel. (Had the old fellow stolen Ziggy's ice cream, or what?) Season ticket holders convened in the "Ziggy Room." When Joe built a gym-nasium on his farm, the Ziggy logo was painted on its roof. (Pilot to co-pilot: "You see what I see?") On Page 16 of the Colonels' game program, 138 words told about Ziggy and his hundreds of dog show victories. On Page 15, there were 79 words about Louie Dampier.

It was March 31, 1967, when the nation's new professional basketball league, the American Basketball Association, introduced itself at a press conference in Oakland, California. Joe, Mamie and Ziggy were there. The husband brought enthusiasm to the project, the wife brought money. An heiress to a family fortune estimated at $50 million, Mamie Spears Reynolds Chinetti Gregory hardly missed the $64,900 necessary to put the Kentucky Colonels into the ABA.

"Joe has taught me everything I know about basketball, which isn't much," she said that day. She was 24 years old. "Oh, I played a bit in grade school. But I always hated it. I couldn't see the point in just throwing a ball so it would fall through a hoop. I've never really been a fan. But I'm willing to learn. And we're going to fill that auditorium on the first night."

Joe and Mamie Gregory with Ziggy, 1967.

Mrs. Gregory once owned a stable of racing cars. "At least 10 cars." The Colonels' game program of Feb. 2, 1968, said that Mamie the Driver "holds several national and international stock car records." After buying a 38-foot boat for $50,000, she traded it in on a 53-foot ocean-going yacht that cost $138,000. She was the daughter of Robert Reynolds, "Our Bob," a U.S. Senator representing North Carolina. Her mother was Evalyn McLean Reynolds, the senator's fifth wife and granddaughter of John R. McLean, who made the family fortune mining gold in Colorado. Among the McLean possessions for a time was the Hope Diamond. Someone asked Mrs. Gregory if that $50 million figure was correct.

"Yes, it is," she said. "A little low, but close."

Mrs. Gregory's formal education was limited. "I went to a Catholic boarding school in Madrid, Spain, for one year. But I didn't go past the eighth grade at Plonk School in Asheville, North Carolina. I didn't care much for school, and my father said travel was just as good anyway."

She earned a master's degree in travel. Seven times she went around the world, stopping long enough in Italy to marry the auto racer Luigi Chinetti, whose father directed the famed Ferrari racing team. The marriage lasted three years. "In your story," she said to a reporter writing about the new basketball team and its owners, "you can just call me a dumb, blonde playgirl."

On Sept. 14, 1965, she both divorced her Italian driver and married Joe Gregory, whom she had hired to train Ziggy. With winnings made on Derby Day, 1947, Gregory, three years out of Cloverport, Ky., High School, bought a Boxer and began a career as a trainer-breeder-judge that in time made him a national figure. Sen. Reynolds befriended Gregory early, retaining him to handle his dogs, and in 1959 Reynolds' 16-year-old daughter Mamie presented a best-in-show trophy to Gregory. It was their first meeting.

Gregory was a basketball addict. He played on his high school team in Cloverport, 70 miles down the Ohio River from Louisville. "I was a fairly decent, fairly good player," he said. He played pickup games while training dogs and was an habitual customer at University of Louisville and UK games. When the Gregorys bought a century-old Shelby County plantation house — "It will become the showplace of Kentucky," Mamie said — one of the first alterations was the addition of the gymnasium next door. Gregory had been reading about Louisville's possible entrance into the ABA. But the potential investors backed out. With just two days notice, Gregory jumped in. His accountant, Bill Motsch, was caught unawares. "How could I say what kind of investment it was?" Motsch said later.

en Joe told me the next day that he'd
ght a team in the ABA, that was the
time I'd ever heard of the ABA. I
't even know what the ABA was."
The accountant was only one of
ral novices on the loose. Making their
selection of players, the Colonels
d on names found in basketball
azines. "Sports Illustrated was a good
" said Bill Boone, the team's lawyer.
Colonels' draft choices somehow
ded a 42-year-old college professor
thought he was too small (at 5 feet
r pro basketball, even in the ABA.
had exclusive rights to him," Boone

Reluctantly, the Colonels made Louie
pier their first player, giving the Uni-
ity of Kentucky All-America a $3,000
s and a $12,000 salary. "They said
didn't think I could play pro ball
use I was too small," Dampier said.
they thought my name and UK might
some tickets." Dampier's signing on
7, 1967, was trumpeted in the Louis-
Times in a two-paragraph story. The
nd paragraph was about two other
ers the Colonels hoped to sign.
The original Colonels' coach was
ny Givens, a former Western Ken-
y University player who had a 29-29
-lost record the three previous years
ew Mexico Highlands College. Early
Givens had trouble, especially with
on Nash. Nash had been a three-time
America at Kentucky. But when he
ed with the Colonels, who lusted after
name, Nash hadn't played basketball
ree years. He was by then a profes-
al baseball player. "I told Cotton that
ad to work if he wanted to play,"
ens said. "He wouldn't do it. Finally,
d him he was just like me, a has-been,
I could beat him one-on-one. So we

played. And, sure enough, I beat him."
Givens tried mightily to motivate
Nash, the team's highest paid player at
$20,000 a year. "Cotton, do you know
who Cassius Clay is?" the coach said.
"Yep," Nash said.
"And do you know who Joe Louis
is?"
"They're both niggers."
"Cotton, they're both world heavyweight boxing champions. And they got
there by working hard, sacrificing, being
dedicated. Joe Louis ran six miles every
day before breakfast. That's what you
have to do, Cotton. Get in shape. Get you
a sweat suit and run every day in Chero-
kee Park."
"Coach," Cotton said gently, "you're
out of your mind."
Nash scored 24 points in a defeat
that first season. "If you play that way
again tomorrow night, we'll win," Givens
said, to which Nash replied, "If you coach
tomorrow night the way you coached
tonight, we'll lose again."
Givens didn't confine his work to the
bench. When a discontented fan in the
upper reaches of the old Convention
Center tossed ice onto the court, Givens
sprinted up an aisle and apprehended
the art critic. It wasn't long until the
Colonels' record dropped to 5-12, and
Givens was replaced with Gene Rhodes,
an assistant coach at Western Kentucky
who had turned down the job when the
Gregorys refused to put his money in
escrow. They relented in the crisis of the
moment, though, and the addition of
Rhodes, a coach of remarkable abilities,
gave a semblance of legitimacy to the
franchise. This *was* the team whose attending doctor was a pediatrician. Dr.
Richard Greathouse, a volunteer, recognized in good humor the incongruity of

his treating pro basketball players. "But, really, the way these guys act, they *are* all babies, aren't they?" he said.

The whole league was five degrees left of sanity. It used a funny red-white-and-blue basketball. A beach ball. "It oughta be on a seal's nose," said Alex Hannum, a coach in the old, established National Basketball Association (who, the year after saying that, signed up with the seal's league). A look at your game program provoked guffaws. The teams' nicknames included the Muskies, Amigos, Pipers, Mavericks and Oaks.

Getting started, Johnny Givens, the Colonels' first coach, talks with Louie Dampier, the team's first player. Note that Givens has a desk. Progress, that is. When he joined the team, he had an office with a phone — and the phone sat on the floor.

In the early years, a coach, Jim Harding, was fired when he won a fist-fight with his team's owner at the All-Star game in Louisville. The Los Angeles Stars hired a belly dancer to lead the players in calisthentics on the premise she helped them develop new muscles. ABA rosters provided refuge to Elton McGriff and Maurice McHartley, DeWitt Menyard and Marlbert Pradd, Justus Thigpen and Dexter Westbrook. Oh, where have you gone, Orb Bowling?

Orb Bowling. An original Colonel. A native of Sandy Hook, Kentucky, 6 feet 10, 215 pounds, a graduate of the University of Tennessee. Slower than a tree. He played in 11 games and averaged 1.9 points a game. When Rhodes took over, he told Bowling he would never play again. That didn't bother Orb, who had a no-cut contract, which meant the Colonels had to pay him his full salary whether he played or not. "I got this here no-cut critter," Bowling said, "so I reckon I'll just hang around." Rhodes didn't take Bowling on road trips. Instead, to please the Colonels' brass, the coach set up a conditioning program for him. Bowling ran in the empty arena at home while the team played a thousand miles away. For home games, Bowling sat on the bench in street clothes.

And there was Howard Bayne, another Tennessee grad. He was 6 feet 6, 235 pounds. His specialty was mayhem. In the NBA then, referees were guided in their calls by the philosophy, "No harm, no foul." In the ABA, it was, "No blood, no foul." Bayne dispensed bruises from Anaheim to Teaneck (that's in New Jersey). He was enthusiastic and determined, but as a pro he had several faults, chief among them being he couldn't play pro basketball. "The funniest thing

I ever saw," Louie Dampier said eight years later, "was the time Howard got a rebound and took off dribbling for the other end. Each dribble, the ball came up higher. And higher. When he got to the other free throw line, the ball was bouncing up over his head. And the last dribble was off his toe." Bayne lasted one season.

The Colonels' usual starting lineup that first year had Dampier and Darel Carrier at guard, Jim Caldwell at center and Jim (Goose) Ligon and Randy Mahaffey at forward. Only Dampier and Carrier

Gene Rhodes suffered exquisitely during a game.

could shoot. "If Goose shot one facing the basket, we said, 'Issue the safety glasses,' because he would chip the backboard," said the suffering Gene Rhodes. "Mahaffey just couldn't see. He wore contacts, but all the time he was squinting and blinking. Caldwell? He was 6-10, 240, he set great picks and he could pass the ball." It became Rhodes' Law that should Dampier and Carrier fail to score 50 points between them, the Colonels couldn't beat Podunk Tech. Considering that the pair's average was 43.5 that year, it's no surprise the Colonels won only 36 of 78 games. Still that was good enough to get them into a playoff game with the New Jersey (Teaneck) Americans. Ah, the good old days.

Because the circus or something had priority on the Teaneck arena, the playoff was moved to Commack, N.Y. "When I saw the Commack place," Rhodes said, "I went into hysterics, I laughed so hard." The floor was pocked with moonlike craters. The goals had been dragged in from a nearby playground. Dampier said, "When we walked in, an old guy was sawing a piece of wood and trying to fit it into a hole about 18 inches by 12 inches. That was the outstanding hole."

Louisville's basketball fans were content without a professional team. Such a venture, tried once in a minor league, failed miserably. The National Basketball Association, established in 1946, was the only major league until in the early '60s Abe Saperstein used his Globetrotter wealth to start the American Basketball League. That league fell apart in less than a year. Cynics suggested that one pro league was boredom enough for the whole nation, what with 140-139 scores every night from October to May. The pros had failed in Louisville, the cynics said, because the town's heart belonged to high school and college basketball.

A lawyer named Wendell Cherry, working on behalf of a wealthy client who considered buying Louisville a team in the latest league, attended organizational meetings in Oakland in 1966. Reporting back, Cherry said, "The American Basketball Association is sheer, absolute nonsense. Only an idiot would get involved."

Several did. Within two years the Pittsburgh Pipers, strapped for operating funds, decided to sell 275,000 shares of stock at $3 a share. A company selling stock to the public is required by law to issue a prospectus, which is a detailed account of assets and liabilities. It shall be nothing but the truth. So the Pipers' prospectus carried a warning in capital letters across the top of the first page: "THE PURCHASE OF SECURITIES OFFERED BY THIS PROSPECTUS SHOULD BE CONSIDERED ONLY BY PERSONS WHO CAN AFFORD TO SUSTAIN A TOTAL LOSS ON THEIR INVESTMENT. THE COMPANY'S OPERATIONS INVOLVE EXTREMELY HIGH RISKS."

Somehow the ABA survived. Tax shelters had something to do with it. A rich guy could lose lots of money in basketball, and then deduct that loss on his income tax — thereby decreasing the income tax he paid on his businesses that were making money. The ABA once was gentlemanly in its dealing with the rival NBA. "Like Boy Scouts playing with the Mafia," Joe Gregory said. But in time the ABA grew aggressive. It stole NBA players. It signed college players, some even before graduation, to contracts that reached as high as $3 million. It established solid organizations around the country, particularly in Indianapolis, Den-

ver, San Antonio, New York and Louisville. Funny. Where did all the idiots go? Who took their places?

Wendell Cherry did, for one. He and four other young, bold Louisville businessmen — Stuart Jay, David Jones, David Grissom and John Y. Brown Jr. — bought the Colonels from Joe Gregory on Oct. 30, 1969. (Mamie didn't like winter time in Louisville and bought a house in Ft. Lauderdale.) "Oh, man, Louisville would go crazy if we won a string of ABA championships," said the converted Cherry.

Immediately, Cherry's group hired general manager/president Mike Storen away from Indianapolis to run the Colonels' operation, giving him free rein. And they drew up a big contract, worth perhaps $1.4 million, to sign Dan Issel, twice an All-America at UK. More than anything else, these three acts — Cherry's purchase of the team, the hiring of Storen and the signing of Issel — made the Colonels a major league outfit. They were signs of commitment to excellence. When the Colonels won their first league championship in May of 1975, Cherry was no longer an owner, Storen was working for the Memphis franchise and two coaches they had hired were gone, too. But Issel was still with the Colonels, and so was Artis Gilmore, a 7-foot-2 center reportedly given a $2.7 million contract by Storen.

Under the Gregorys, without whom Louisville would never have had the Colonels, the basketball team ran on nickels and pennies. "They were supposed to have all this money," Givens said. "But nobody ever saw it." Rhodes said, "We never could improve our personnel. We had good people and they tried hard. But Bill Motsch had access to the league books, and he didn't think the league was going to make it. So he wasn't

In 1969 these men bought the Colonels. From left: Stuart Jay, Wendell Cherry, David Grissom, David Jones, John Y. Brown.

going to let the Gregorys put any more money into it than they had to. When we signed Wayne Chapman the second year for $25,000 a year, I thought they were going to have a stroke." For $7,000 in bonuses, Rhodes said, the Colonels could have signed both Greg Smith and Bob Dandridge, who went instead to Milwaukee of the NBA where they were starters on a world championship team. The Colonels also failed to sign Westley Unseld, a two-time All-America at Louisville.

Cherry and Storen wasted no time. Even before Storen left Indianapolis to begin work officially for the Colonels, he advised Cherry to get Issel at any cost. That, he did. During the negotiations, John Y. Brown Jr., one of the five partners, stormed out of the room. Brown had made millions building Kentucky Fried Chicken and Colonel Harland Sanders into a world-wide enterprise. "Hell," he said of Issel's demands, "that's more than we pay the Colonel."

With Storen in charge, the Colonels were, to use a newspaperman's term, good copy. Storen was arrogant, abrasive, powerful, charming, egotistical. Asked once if he could, without bragging

on himself, tell how much he had to do with the success of the Indiana Pacers, who twice were league champions and No. 1 in attendance every year, Storen said forcefully, "I had total authority." Over players, too? "Total authority," he said. Storen transformed the Colonels from one owner's toy into another's moving and shaking business. "We have eliminated Ziggy," Storen said at a press conference called to unveil a new, modernistic logo featuring an ABA basketball (which ball, by the way, was the brainchild of Storen; he owned merchandising rights to it, and was made richer with the sale of each once-scorned beach ball).

Only 15 games into Storen's first season, he fired Gene Rhodes as coach and replaced him with Frank Ramsey. It was a trying time, for Rhodes was popular in Louisville, where he'd been first a star player at Male High and later an outstanding coach at St. Xavier and Male. Storen told a newspaperman he couldn't discuss why Rhodes had been fired because to do so would only cause the coach "irreparable" damage. For that one, Rhodes sued Storen and the Colonels—and won a cash settlement,

Mike Storen sometimes didn't like referees.

Frank Ramsey coached the Colonels in 1971.

the amount undisclosed.

That was only the beginning. As part of the fallout from the Rhodes firing, Storen said he'd received threatening phone calls. He said he'd asked the police to guard his house. Later that season, Ramsey was accused by the team trainer, on Page One of the Louisville Times, of not knowing his business. The trainer, Bill Antonini, admitted he was "slightly" inebriated when he made the remarks, but he didn't deny them. He also said the team was beset by racial dissension. A newspaper story quoted an unnamed player as saying Ramsey sometimes asked the players during timeouts what should be done next. Storen held a team meeting to find out who said that. "He said he was going to keep us there all night, until the guy who said it admitted it," Louie Dampier said. "So I told him I said it." With Dampier's confession of the innocent quote, he was replaced as captain of the team by Cincy Powell.

Meanwhile, on the playing floor, the Colonels, with the rookie Issel averaging 29.9 points as a center, moved to the seventh and decisive game of the league championships. There they lost to Utah. But no one really minded much, for the next season Artis Gilmore would be in uniform — and wouldn't he make a one-game difference?

As it happened, the Colonels won 68 regular-season games and lost only 16 in Gilmore's rookie season, a league record. The coach then was Joe Mullaney (Ramsey had quit of his own accord). Certain of Gilmore's limitations — Mullaney always thought the big guy could neither catch nor pass the ball well enough to be an integral part of a balanced offense — Mullaney built an offense designed to give Gilmore and Issel the ball near the basket. By playoff time, everybody this side of the Iron Curtain knew where the ball went on every Colonels play — and New York eliminated Kentucky in the first round of the playoffs.

The next season, 1972-73, the Colonels again lost in the seventh game of the championship round, that time to the cursed Indiana Pacers, their Interstate-65 rivals. Owner Wendell Cherry, who rapidly was losing money and enthusiasm, worked a deal to sell the Colonels to people in Cincinnati. John Y. Brown Jr. was eating dinner at home one night when his son, John III, 10 years old, said, "Daddy, you haven't really sold the Colonels, have you?"

Well, what does a multi-millionaire do when his son weeps at the dinner table over the loss of his favorite team?

Exactly.

"I don't think I'd been to 10 games myself, and I'd lost $100,000," Brown said. "That's a right expensive ticket. But when John cried, I figured maybe a lot of people in Louisville felt the same way."

So Brown bought back from Cincinnati 51 per cent of the Colonels. Rather, his wife, Ellie, did. She was introduced as the majority stockholder. It was a masterstroke of public relations. Ellie Brown suddenly appeared on national television with Dinah Shore and Howard Cosell. She was on "Today" and "What's My Line?" Meanwhile, her husband fired Joe Mullaney ("What would you do if you paid $2 million for a team and the coach told you it wasn't any good?" said Dave Vance, then the team's publicity man). Brown hired Babe McCarthy to replace Mullaney.

The Colonels were eliminated in the second round of the playoffs by the

When Ramsey quit, the Colonels hired Joe Mullaney.

eventual champions, the New York Nets. The defeat, in four straight games, was made more bitter by a midseason trade drawn up by owner Brown. He sent two starters, Mike Gale and Wendell Ladner, to New York in exchange for John Roche, who wound up a second-stringer for the Colonels. Brown had made the deal without consulting his coach. When the Nets pushed the Colonels out of the playoffs, Ladner, a wonderfully wacky Mississippian whose antics had made him a favorite of the Colonels' fans (once, chasing a loose ball, he slid to a stop next to a cheerleader and said, "Meet me after the game"; another time he dove into a glass water cooler and was sliced up so badly that it took 54 stitches to put him together, but as he arose, bleeding, his concern was his handsome appearance: "Is mah hair mess up?") — anyway, Ladner stood at center court after the Nets victory and waved at John and Ellie Brown. They tried to smile.

For the 1974-75 season, Brown transformed his team. He said it was his son John's advice that led to the purchase of guard Ted McClain. He also bought

forward Marv Roberts and guard Bird Averitt. He signed forward Wil Jones as a free agent at $100,000 a year. And he hired Hubie Brown to coach, bringing him to Kentucky from an assistant's job with the Milwaukee Bucks of the NBA.

As always, Louie Dampier played. Issel and Gilmore, too. But, suddenly, that threesome had a whole lot of help, and by playoff time the Colonels clearly were the strongest team in the league. Under coach Brown's direction, Gilmore improved offensively more in that season than he had in the three previous. Issel

Ellie and John Y. Brown Jr., 1973.

168

was asked to do a true forward's job — facing the basket, moving in the offense, passing the ball, instead of simply setting up near the basket as he'd done for Mullaney — and he played superbly in a string of important games at season's end.

But it was Dampier more than anyone who came to symbolize the Colonels' arrival at the top. The original Colonel, the one they signed for $12,000 because his name might sell some tickets, the one who owner Brown thought was too old — "They wanted me to take a $10,000 pay cut," said Dampier, who for the first time retained an agent and wound up with a $10,000 raise and a two-year contract worth $120,000 — Louie Dampier at age 30, in his eighth season as a pro, played the best basketball of his life. Hubie Brown, an analytical, tutorial kind of coach, said, "Louie Dampier can play basketball anywhere. He could be an outstanding asset to *any* league, *any* team, *any* place. . . He's a pro's pro, and that's the highest compliment I can give him. He has the natural ability to want the last shot, the tremendous confidence in his shooting to win the pressure game. . . . If he played on a team with Jerry West or Nate Archibald or Walt Frazier — those guys who take two people to guard them — Louis Dampier would be a household name across the country. He would be a consistent 20-plus scorer and probably would be referred to as one of the greatest jump shooters from 17 to 25 feet ever to play the game."

Dampier shot 51 per cent on two-pointers in '74-75, and he made 39.6 per cent of his three-point tries. Never had he done better. He averaged 16.8 points a game, making his career average 19.6. He had 449 assists and only 146 errors,

an astounding 3-to-1 ratio in a time when a guard is considered a competent ball-handler if his assists even double his mistakes. Dampier, at 6 feet, led the ABA guards in blocked shots with 53. Only 18 players, counting all those high-rise pituitary accidents, blocked more. As long as we're dealing with numbers, let's get these in — Dampier held the team scoring record of 55 points; he once made 9 of 11 three-point attempts in a game; he held the league record of 58 straight free throws; through 1975, he was the ABA's all-time leading scorer with 12,656 points, and he'd played 24,935 minutes in 646 regular-season games. That's 38.6 minutes a night for eight years. Late in the '75 season, he had 17 stitches taken in his hand, and he grouched the next night because Brown wouldn't let him play. "The great ones want the last shot," the coach said. "They play in the All-Star games, and Louie's been in seven of them. And they play with pain. Louie has missed seven games in eight years."

If the Colonels' patrons stood in awe of Artis Gilmore, if they cheered madly for Dan Issel (and hissed when owner Brown sold the big guy), if they momentarily lost their heads in an infatuation with Wendell Ladner, always they loved Louie Dampier. "I'm convinced he's No. 1 with our fans," said Dave Vance, the Colonels general manager. "I've run my private survey. I've asked people what player, if we sold or traded him, would have the greatest negative impact on the community. Unanimously, the answer has been Louie." Why? "He's just Little Louie, that's all."

Dampier worked without affectation. On the court, he did his job straightforwardly, pure and simple. First he was

Louie Dampier from 20 feet.

a beautiful shooter. "God taught Louie how to shoot," Adolph Rupp once said, "and I took credit for it." Then Dampier became a competent passer and, finally, a defensive player of persistence. What endeared him to the customers, though, was not his flawless performance; it was his innocence. In a day of high visibility for pro athletes, when attention came easily and brought with it inflated egos, Dampier was unmoved by his stardom. One television commercial was proof certain. In connection with a hamburger outfit, Dampier came to kiss a costumed character called Queenie Bee. He did it with a little-boy grin of embarrassment. Leers belonged to Joe Namath and his panty hose.

Dampier liked privacy. He cut his own hair. He drove an economy car. Given a choice on television, he'd watch a comedy before a news special. He bought a 60-year-old house in suburban Louisville and renovated it himself. During the summer, he played softball for a team called the Heffalumps. The portrait is of Everyman.

Until Dampier was a junior at Southport High School, near Indianapolis, he was 5 feet 2 and couldn't shoot a jump shot. He grew eight inches that summer. His senior year his scoring average went from 11 points a game to 25. Both Indiana University and Kentucky recruited him. "The Indiana coach was Branch Mc-Cracken and when I went there for a visit, he kinda ignored me the whole day," Dampier said. "At Kentucky, they made me feel wanted."

Rupp had been to Southport to see Dampier play. "I made nine out of 10 shots the first half, and Rupp left. He said he'd seen enough," Dampier said. His three seasons at UK were a curious mix-

ture. As a sophomore, Dampier started on a team that won 15 games and lost 10 — Rupp's worst record ever.

The next season, 1965-66, belonged to "Rupp's Runts." Dampier and Tommy Kron were the guards. Thad Jaracz was the center (at 6 feet 5, he and Kron were the team's biggest starters). Pat Riley and Larry Conley were the forwards. Kentucky won its first 23 games. Its size and remarkably precise ballhandling captivated people across the country. At season's end, Dampier and Riley, both All-Americas, received 300 letters of praise in 10 days. "All of us just melded together that year," Dampier said. "And Rupp seemed healthier that season. He was into the coaching more than he had been."

Texas Western defeated the Runts in the NCAA championship game. "Conley was sick, and Riley had a bad toe, and Jaracz was under the weather, too," Dampier said. "The game was tough. Texas Western played defense more aggressively than other schools. And we weren't as fired up for that game as we had been for Duke in the semifinals. We were rated No. 1 and Duke No. 2. When we won that one, we figured that was it."

Dampier's senior season, UK finished 13-13, primarily because Riley played with a slipped disc in his back and was a pathetic caricature of the previous year's strong and graceful athlete.

So much happens so quickly in a basketball game that it's foolhardy to pick a moment and say this is it — this is the very second the Kentucky Colonels won the American Basketball Association. We'll do it anyway, for if Artis Gilmore's 10-foot hook shot didn't guarantee victory on May 22, 1975, it did send 16,622

Dampier sails past Chuck Williams of San Diego.

crazies into screaming orbit inside Freedom Hall. Wendell Cherry knew what he was talking about.

Gilmore's hook shot, sent ever-so-softly goalward, bumped against the back of the rim and came forward. There it hung on the front edge, its destination unknown. At last, maybe three days later, it fell into the net — and the Colonels led the Indiana Pacers 104 to 97. Less than two minutes were left in the game, and that basket did it. The Colonels won 110-105, taking the best-of-seven series four games to one.

In the madness of the subsequent celebration that night, time had repaid a debt to Gene Rhodes, once the Colonels' coach and — is this poetic justice? — then hired to replace Mike Storen as the team's general manager. "We've come a long way since Ziggy," Rhodes said. "This sure beats the hell out of going down the tube every night at Convention Center."

For the Colonels, the championship was redemption. Twice in the previous four seasons, the team made it to the seventh and deciding game of the championship series — only to lose. Of

The Dampiers, Louie and Marty with Nick and Danielle, 1973.

172

such calamities is born the melancholy reputation as a loser, a choker. No one had a chance to speak those cutting words in 1975, for the Colonels were awesome in the three playoff rounds, using only 15 games to win the necessary 12. Dan Issel, then in his fifth season, had played in all the Colonels' championship series. What was different the last time?

"We just have more talent now," he said. He sat at courtside as Gov. Julian Carroll and Ellie Brown moved to midcourt for a trophy presentation. From the roof of the arena came a chant, "We want Dan. We want Dan." Issel's wife, Cheri, looked at her man and they shared a smile. "The biggest difference was on defense," Issel said. "Hubie Brown taught us how to play defense."

Someone asked Louie Dampier what the difference was between the other seasons and 1975.

"We won," he said with a smile that lit the dark corners of Freedom Hall. "We played well all year under pressure, especially at the end. This is a better team than we've ever had. We definitely were the strongest team in the league."

But weren't the Colonels the strongest in other years — and didn't win?

"I thought we were the best in Artis' first year, when we only lost 16 games, but New York beat us in the first round then. The difference is coaching, plus the personnel we've picked up this year." It was Dampier's first major championship at any level of basketball. How did he feel? "I'm stunned right now. Ask me in an hour."

All around Dampier the place was up for grabs. Fans dodged policemen to give Issel a hug. They chased Dampier for his autograph. Marty Dampier, once a cheerleader at Southport High, kissed her husband. A leaping man threw confetti on Gilmore's head. Assistant coach Stan Albeck whacked forward Ron Thomas on the rump with a clipboard. Gov. Carroll spoke into a microphone, saying he was thrilled. Ellie Brown praised the Pacers. Hubie Brown thanked God. Someone asked Ellie's husband, John Y. Brown Jr., if such a celebration was what he wanted when the Browns bought the team two years earlier. "I imagine," he said with a laugh.

John Y. Brown III, whose tears kept the Colonels in Louisville, said, "I'm *very* happy." He said Artis Gilmore won it. "He's the biggest thing around," John III said.

Gilmore had 28 points and 31 rebounds that night, a third majestic performance in the series. It earned him the playoffs' Most Valuable Player award. And in the process, it affirmed the coaching genius of Hubie Brown. In other playoff games in other years, Artis Gilmore had been less than majestic. For the change, Brown deserved credit. He brought precision to Gilmore, and to the Colonels.

Brown brought a pro's cool, too. In the last frenetic minutes of the game the Colonels had been trying to win for eight years — in that time when the Pacers were three points behind and threatening — Brown in the timeout huddle was, as always, a stern, controlled teacher. "Relax now, guys," he said. "Meet the passes. Come out and get them. Now, if we lose the ball, get back on defense quick." Panic owned no part of Brown, nor of his team, and with 15 seconds to play Gilmore made two free throws for the final 110-105 score.

A reporter that night called Joe Gregory in Ft. Lauderdale. The original

owner of the Colonels, the first fan. "He'd have liked nothing better than to coach the team himself," said Bill Boone, the lawyer. Gregory's wife, Mamie, once was so upset with the Colonels' performance that she charged into the locker room. Players were dressed the way players usually are dressed after a game. Nakedly. "She was so mad she didn't even notice," said Ed Kallay, the team's radio announcer. The Gregorys brought the pros to Louisville when no one else would. And they cared mightily. And when a reporter talked to Joe about the 1975 championship, Gregory said, "I'm sure glad we won and finally achieved what we started out to do." Gregory also said Ziggy died about a year before of old age.

Hey, this is fun. Gilmore is ready to start the fast break.

Hubie Brown and Artis Gilmore.

Celebrating. From left: Ellie Brown, Bird Averitt, assistant coach Stan Albeck and trainer Lloyd Gardner are happy moments after the Colonels won the 1975 ABA championship.

THE GREAT ARBITRATOR AND LOUISVILLE GATES

In the Maya Indian City of Tikal, buried deep in the jungles of Guatemala in tropical Central America, archeologists discovered that basketball was played long before James Naismith had Mr. Stebbins tack up those peach baskets. With seven men on a team, games of "pok a tok" lasted from sunrise to sunset, sometimes for several days. The field was 480 feet long, 120 feet wide and enclosed by stone walls 28 feet high. At each end was a temple directly behind a massive stone ring four feet in diameter and 20 feet off the ground. A solid-rubber ball was to be thrown through the two-foot openings in the rings. At game's end, the captain of the losing team marched in a great ceremonial procession to one of the temples, where he placed his head on an execution block. The winning captain, using a stone knife, made the victory official. People have been losing their heads over basketball ever since.

☛ Dr. Robert L. McGeachin was a professor of biochemistry at the University of Louisville. He and his wife, Margaret, could be described as extraordinary fans of the Louisville Cardinals basketball team. Mrs. McGeachin attended road games with a cardinal in her hair.

"It's housebroken," she said.

It was also a stuffed toy.

"I keep it in a plastic bag in my dresser drawer. It's my second one, actually. The first one wore out. Its tail feathers fell out."

☛ Joe Hall, the Kentucky coach, remembered a legendary UK rooter.

"He was 85 years old, from Somerset, and he had a crippled leg. He'd walk from his place in the country to a road where he'd flag down a bus into Somerset.

"Then he'd catch a bus to Lexington and take a nap in the bus station until it was time to go to the Coliseum for the game.

"After the game, he'd walk back to the bus station and sleep there until 3 or 4 o'clock in the morning. He'd catch another bus back to Somerset and walk home. It was about a 24-hour deal for him to come to a UK game."

Did he come often?

Every game."

This was the day before UK played in the 1975 NCAA semifinals at San Diego. Would the old boy be in San Diego?

"No, he's dead," Hall said.

A sports writer put that story in the paper. A letter arrived shortly. "This article was incorrect and a little premature," said Mrs. Edward Buis of Waynesburg, Ky. "The old fellow...did watch the NCAA games! He is Simeon J. Hale and is now 91 years old and very much alive ... P. S. Mr. Hale has been to three UK home games this season!"

☛ Webb Cook, 10, wasn't impressed when his father, U.S. Senator Marlow Cook, a Republican from Louisville, served as master of ceremonies at Rich-

Joy

Fans fill up Freedom Hall for an NCAA Tournament.

ard Nixon's 1972 inauguration.

"I just want to get home and play basketball," the young Cook said. "You know, I missed practice today just because of this inauguration."

☛ Martin Fallon, a member of the Monsignor Newman chapter of the Knights of Columbus, was driving a truck west on Louisville's Watterson Expressway on Dec. 21, 1974, carrying a variety of items to fill Christmas baskets for the needy.

A box containing a dozen red-white-and-blue basketballs, tied to the top of the truck, broke loose. When Fallon stopped to retrieve the balls, two men in a white car also stopped, grabbed the box and fled.

☛ Tommy Puckett, a policeman from Lexington, was scheduled to marry Julie Gaskin at 3 p.m., March 29, 1975. The invitations were in the mail when a crisis came up. UK's basketball team won its way to the NCAA semifinals, where it would play Syracuse — at 3 p.m. March 29.

With Julie's consent, Puckett sent the wedding guests postcards bearing the picture of a basketball player. He changed the time to 2 p.m. and added a note: "UK is No. 1, Puckett-Gaskin Wedding No. 2. See you at the church and tip-off, too. Julie and Tommy."

☛ It happened at Salyersville in the late 1940's. Sid Meade, who refereed in Kentucky for 35 years, was in the gymnasium restroom, resting. A man walked up to him. He had a pistol in his hand.

"Look, ref," the man said. "I've got my mustering-out pay on this game, and the complexion of this game had better change."

The hometown Salyersville team, undefeated that year, was four points behind Sandy Hook at halftime.

"Mister," Meade said, "you don't have money enough to buy me, or guns enough to scare me. So get out of here."

Well, Sid, what happened in the second half?

"Don't you know that Salyersville came back to win that game at the free-pitch line," Meade said.

☛ On March 14, 1974, State Rep. Terry McBrayer was supposed to be in Frankfort for a session of the General Assembly. Instead, he was at the State Tournament, seated in the Greenup County High School section, cheering madly for the Musketeers against Fleming County.

"I think they'll forgive me," said McBrayer, a former Greenup player. "They know that coming to the State Tournament with your home team is more important than passing legislation."

☛ At center court in Madison Square Garden, Muhammad Ali, the world heavyweight boxing champion, stopped a practice of Manhattan College. "Give me a ball, my man," he said. And with a right-handed hook shot from 45 feet, Ali banked the ball through the hoop. This miracle caused someone to ask if Ali played basketball as a youngster in Louisville. "Nope," he said. "But if I did, I would have been the *greatest*!"

☛ Hired from Kansas State, Steve Goldman came to work as an assistant football coach at the University of Louisville in the winter of 1975. Was he impressed by basketball in Louisville? "My boy was out in the street throwing a *football* around," Goldman said. "And the police *arrested* him."

☛ Ford Reid, a Courier-Journal and Louisville Times photographer, was a basketball freak. With a friend named Bill Pike, Reid proposed to revolutionize the game. "Our idea," Reid said, "was to

How to be two places at once.

recess the key, with sloping sides, and all the guys 6-8 or over would have to play in there. The closer you get to the basket, the deeper it gets.

"Then, when a team is ahead by 10 points, the basket starts to move back and forth across the backboard. If it gets ahead by 20, the basket moves back and forth and up and down. This would be electronically controlled random movement, so you couldn't figure out what it was going to do next."

"We also thought there should be those sliding floors, like they have in fun houses. That would slow people down and put some unpredictability into it. There would have to be another official. We call him the Great Arbitrator. There would be an electronic device in the ball, and he would control it with a wand at the table.

"Imagine guys on a fast break. A long pass is thrown, but when the ball hits the floor, it just goes dead. Stops. Then, as everybody scrambles for the ball, the G.A. could make it go straight up in the air and the floor would start moving back and forth." Here Reid stopped to laugh.

"That would put an end to dull basketball. Even if a team was ahead 90-31, people would stick around to see what the Great Arbitrator would take a notion to do."

☛ In the greatest coup of a career full of remarkable achievements, a gate crasher from Louisville wound up with a front-row center seat for the UCLA-North Carolina State basketball game in March of 1974 while thousands of Carolinians stayed at home.

Let's call this fellow "Louisville Gates." With five accomplices, Gates went to Greensboro without a single ticket for the NCAA semifinal games. By tipoff time, he had not one ticket — he had *nine*.

Tickets went on sale by mail April 1, 1973. At noon that day, 80,000 letters had arrived. Only 4,000 tickets were available. Stories in the Greensboro newspapers reported scalpers sold $20 tickets for $200.

Did that scalping price bother Gates? "Hrrumph," he said.

Gates had a long history of attending sporting events where tickets were not available. Of several techniques, his favorite was "machine-gunning." As he approached a ticket taker, he flashed a

Defeat.

badge in his wallet — very quickly, at about the speed bullets leave a machine gun. Doing that, Gates also mumbled a lot.

"They somehow think I'm the governor's bodyguard," Gates said. The badge was his old St. Francis of Assisi schoolboy patrol badge.

He had been to Super Bowls, to a heavyweight championship fight, to the World Series. Most often he paid his way in. "But never more than the regular ticket price," he said proudly.

For the NCAA semifinal game matching top-ranked N.C. State and perennial champion UCLA, Gates was operating at his best.

His seat was next to Dr. Archie Dykes, the chancellor of Kansas University. Two of Gates' accomplices sat four rows from courtside, just three seats over from Bob Knight, the Indiana University coach. How Gates did it was a dramatic story of human resourcefulness.

First he took up a station in the lobby of the Hilton Inn on Friday night.

There he spotted Ken Trickey, who recently had resigned as coach at Oral Roberts University. During the Midwest Regionals, Trickey had been arrested for drunken driving, a development hardly in keeping with his evangelistic boss's reputation.

"Coach, I'm a fan of yours," Gates said. "I'm a lawyer from Louisville. I think you got a bad rap, and I'll come out and defend you for free."

Whereupon they retired to the bar to talk over the case.

Result: Two tickets from Trickey.

Saturday morning in the Hilton lobby, Gates noticed a man leave an envelope full of NCAA tickets at the front desk. It was 9:30 a.m. At 11:15 a.m., barely two hours before the first semifinal game,

Faith.

Gates made a move.

"Excuse me, sir," he said. "I don't mean to butt into your business. But I noticed you left some tickets at the desk — and no one had picked them up yet. Do you think your man might not be showing up?"

A phone call to Myrtle Beach, South Carolina, confirmed that the man's friend couldn't make it to Greensboro. "Hey, you're pretty sharp," the man said to Gates, who said in return, "I'll take two."

This was a simultaneous action. While keeping an eye on that precious envelope at the desk, Gates worked another field. He saw lots of Kansas University supporters (their team was to play Marquette). They were identifiable by colorful Jayhawk insignias on their lapels.

"So I got me a Jayhawk — to show my allegiance," Gates said.

He talked to his fellow Jayhawkers. One was the school's assistant sports information director. Why, yes, he had a couple extra tickets. Gates later talked a ticket out of a man on his way to the buffet table.

"He was the Kansas president," Gates said. "He said he had a seat right next to his and I was welcome to it. I said thank you."

That was seven tickets. An accomplice brought in two more from Hugh Durham, the coach at Florida State and a Louisville native.

What did Gates do with nine tickets when he needed only six?

"We scalped three of 'em and made our expenses for the trip down here," he said.

THE GIRLS PLAY BASKETBALL, TOO

Back when the world was young, an anvil-footed playmaker sat with a pretty girl in a car late one night. When not otherwise occupied, they talked.

"I played basketball once," she said.

"You did?"

"For our church team," she said.

"How'd you do?"

"Oh, I scored all our points."

"*All* of them?" The playmaker, who never scored 20 points in a game, was impressed. "How many did you get?"

"We weren't very good," the pretty one said. "It was our first game, and it was a big tournament, and we played against the champion team."

"How many points did you get?"

"Fourteen," she said.

Alas, the playmaker laughed. Out loud. "You scored *all* your team's points, and 14 was *all* you got?" The playmaker would live to regret those words.

"We were just a new team," she said coolly.

"Did you win?"

"We lost."

Maybe it was his imagination, but the playmaker sensed a chill in the air. "What was the score?" he said.

"That's not important." An Arctic breeze moved through the car.

"Come on," he said.

"If you *must* know, it was 72-14," she said. By a miracle of meteorology, icicles formed on the rear-view mirror. For years afterward, the bonds of wedded bliss could be tested for their strength by the use of that score, as in, "Hmmm, 72-14 wasn't it?"

Girls played basketball from the start in 1891. Happy Chandler and Ed Diddle coached college girl teams in Kentucky. The high school girls played a State Tournament until 1932 when the powers-that-were discontinued the game for either the public reason (too hard on the poor little dears) or the whispered reason (the men in charge mixed hanky-panky with coaching). But in 1974 the Kentucky state legislature required all high schools to have girls basketball if the girls wanted it. And 304 schools had teams. Earlington High was one of them.

Earlington, January, 1975.

The Earl's Stand & Rack is Earlington's only newsstand and book rack. It's on South Railroad Street, three doors from the town's traffic light. The manager is Garth Gamblin, and if you want to know what's happening in Earlington, you ask Garth.

So how's the girls basketball team doing?

"Haven't won a game," Gamblin said.

Do you know anything else about the team?

"Only that they ain't worth a dime."

Earlington is an old coal town of about 2,800 people. It's six miles from Madisonville. Basketball always has been big here. The boys won the State Tourna-

While Diddle coached at Western, A. B. (Happy) Chandler coached the University of Kentucky girls basketball team. The future Governor and U.S. Senator stands with (from left) Margaret Ligon, Antoinette Harrison, Sarah Blanding (later president of Vassar College), Miss Thompson and Elizabeth Carroll.

Diddle (right) coached the Western Kentucky girls basketball team. He wound up marrying his All-State forward, Margaret Louise Monin (third from left).

ment in 1967. "Used to be, every kid had a basketball in his hand," said Kenneth Hayes, who runs a grocery store. "And they all had goals out in the backyard."

Hayes said it's nice the girls have a team. "Times change," he said, "and we have to change, too, or get left behind." But the grocer's enthusiasm for girls basketball is small. "They got a home ec teacher or somethin' to coach 'em. She don't know anything about coachin' ball."

Earlington High has lost its first 10 games by an average score of 56-20. One defeat was 70-9. The coach is Francis Bibb, who teaches remedial mathematics, not home ec, for grades 1-4. Back in 1932, things were better. Earlington went to the semifinals of the State Tournament when the team star was Elizabeth Coffman, now a teacher at Earlington High. "They quit playing girls ball, they said, because it was too strenuous for the girls," Mrs. Coffman said. "I think it's good exercise."

Francis Bibb sees benefits far beyond exercise. She believes basketball is a step toward fulfillment of a girl's potential as a woman. With little urging, she is evangelistic about it.

"The girls become more confident, they develop a new awareness," Miss Bibb said. "They feel emotions they've never even noticed before. They begin to find out things about themselves.

"I have some girls who always had been very quiet. One hid in corners. Walking down the hall at school, she'd press against the wall. They've begun to come out of their shells, to be more interested in themselves. They've begun to look at things with a different perspective. They're looking for challenges now."

The first challenge accepted by the Earlington girls was — how do you dribble a basketball without breaking your leg?

"None of these girls had *ever* played basketball," said Miss Bibb, 22, who learned basketball "in the backyard, playing knock-down, drag-out with my two brothers in Central City."

So what was the first thing the coach taught the Earlington girls?

"Well, like, 'This is a basketball, and that's a goal,'" Miss Bibb said. "I looked to find out what they could do. And I found out in a hurry."

What could they do?

"Nothin'."

Miss Bibb laughed a lot, talking about her girls. Recruited from the Earlington grade school to coach the high school team — "They knew my father was coaching, and I was single, so I'd have the time" — she is having fun. Even mention of the 70-9 cataclysm produces a smile.

"Oooh, man," she said. "But we're getting better."

Jim Larmouth, once the Earlington boys coach and now the high school superintendent, noticed the improvement. "They're not double-dribbling all the time now," he said.

Larmouth was in his office with Lige Shadowen, the high school principal and once a star player at Crittenden County High. When a newspaperman said he was in town to do a story on the girls team, Shadowen rolled his eyes and walked out of Larmouth's office.

Taking a wild guess, does that retreat mean the principal is less than ecstatic about girls basketball?

"It's been something of a pain to him," Larmouth said.

Shadowen returned. He confirmed the pain. "They can sit up in the legislature and pass these laws and say you have to play girls basketball and you have to fund it and..." Shadowen let the sentence die,

Francis Bibb, the Earlington girls' coach, is ready for a game against Bremen High, coached by her father, Thomas (at right).

its conclusion made obvious by the dark cloud settling over his brow.

The principal recited a litany of complaints about the girls. He said that Miss Bibb scheduled too many good teams — that she should have played weaker ones in this first season. He said the best box-office profit at four home games has been $50, one-fourth what the boys made. He said the average crowd for a girls game is 100 people.

"And she," Shadowen said, speaking of Miss Bibb without using her name, "wants everything equal — equipment, uniforms, trophies, everything."

Someone mentioned that girls basketball is big in Iowa, where the girls state tournament draws 10,000 paying customers and rates Second Coming play in the newspapers.

"It's going to be a long time before that happens here," Shadowen said. It was hard to tell if that was a prediction or a threat.

The Earlington High boys coach, Bob McCord, also contains his excitement over girls basketball.

"They can take that politician who passed the law and hang him," McCord said.

"He didn't think of dressing rooms. When the girls play games preceding the boys games — and here in Hopkins County, we have to play eight girls games in front of the boys — we need to stand somebody outside the dressing room door until the girls are done.

"He didn't think of a girls coach's salary, which is the same as my assistant coach's. He didn't think of bus trips, about $50 a trip for 10 or 15 trips. He didn't think of uniforms — and she's spent maybe $200 or $250 on uniforms."

Again, the unidentified "she" is Miss Bibb.

"The whole thing," McCord said, "probably cost the school $1,000 — and it came out of the athletic fund, which is money mostly brought in by boys basketball."

Miss Bibb is not without allies. Her father, for one. Thomas Bibb coaches the girls team at Bremen High, and his team played his daughter's team the other night.

"I pay just as much tax for my two girls as I do for my two boys," he said, "and if my boys can play in a good gym

Karen Hornik of Louisville Doss goes after the ball.

built with my tax money, so can my girls."

In the end, Miss Bibb is her own best defender.

What about principal Shadowen's complaints about the girls team?

"Being a typical man, he's interested in getting all he can for the boys," she said sweetly, smiling.

And it seems McCord, the boys coach, doesn't much like the girls coach.

"That's because I'm bigger than he is," Miss Bibb said sweetly, smiling. She is 5 feet 8, McCord is about 5-6.

As for the father-daughter game, Bremen against Earlington, Earlington's best defense was a chorus of screams from the bench when Bremen shot a free throw. On offense, Earlington's best play was a jump ball. Bremen won 31-30, and Miss Bibb said, "We're getting better."

The 1975 girls State Tournament drew 22,917 spectators, paying $44,384. Joe Billy Mansfield, Commissioner of the Kentucky High School Athletic Association, said, "It really went over better than we expected. I was afraid it would be a disaster. I'm pleasantly surprised."

So was Brian Harvey, 15, a varsity player at Waggener High in Louisville, surprised by girls basketball. "I think it's fun watching 'em," he said to someone who wondered why a guy showed up two hours before his game to watch girls play the preliminary.

Harvey studied the action intently.

"I like that No. 11," he said, pointing out a left-hander whose 15-foot jump shot had failed.

What did he like about her?

"She's good-looking, for one thing."

Girls basketball was all right with Harvey. "I like the spirit, the yelling and cheering the girls do for each other. The cheering during warmups, that's really weird!"

The varsity player's devotion to girls basketball — or to *girls* and *basketball* — is such that he'd make the ultimate sacrifice.

"If it wasn't for our games following right behind the girls games, I'd be a cheerleader for the girls. I really would."

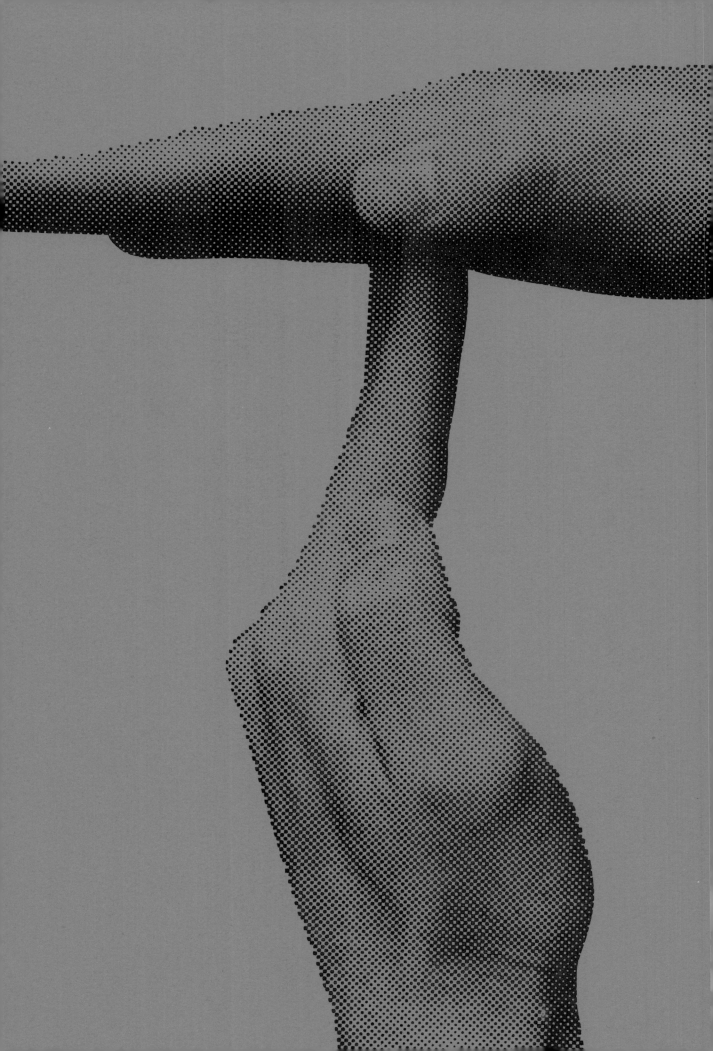

ARE YOU READY, ST. PETER?

Author's note: In doing research for this last chapter, I asked several coaches to help me pick the 10 best players ever to suit up for Kentucky colleges. Invariably, the coaches looked at me real funny. It was impossible, they said. Too many good players. They said anybody with half a brain wouldn't even try to do it. That didn't rule me out, of course, so I interviewed myself.

Question: Did you ask Adolph Rupp?

Answer: I was working up to it. First I asked him this: "Coach, if you were playing a game to save the world, which man would you want on your team — Frank Ramsey or Cliff Hagan?" You'd have thought I wanted the combination to his money belt. "Good gawd no, I won't answer *that*," Adolph said. So I dropped the subject.

Q. Rupp never named his all-time best, did he?

A. Nope. One time he did describe the composite UK player. That marvelous creature, in Rupp's words, would have "the shooting eye of Larry Pursiful and Louie Dampier, the drive of Frank Ramsey, the speed of Ralph Beard and Ronnie Lyons, the grace of Cliff Hagan, the de-

fensive ability of Billy Evans and Kenny Rollins, the temperament of Aggie Sale, the rebounding ability of Bob Burrow, the passing wizardry of Cliff Barker, the competitive spirit of Wah-Wah Jones, the scholastic ability of Jim McDonald, the hands of Cotton Nash and the scoring ability of Dan Issel."

Q. If Rupp won't name his best players, what makes you think you can?

A. Rupp was being diplomatic. He didn't want to name some players and leave others off. That's the practical approach. But I'm not practical. Like when I was a kid. We'd make up crazy questions. Could an all-star team of second basemen, if they had Sandy Koufax pitching, beat the 1927 Yankees? Would Ty Cobb have dared spike Jackie Robinson? How far could Johnny Unitas throw a baseball? How many days could Annette Funicello keep a hula hoop going?

Q. Questions with no answers, right?

A. No answers, just debates. That's what I wanted the coaches to help me with, just one question: If we're going to play St. Peter's All-Stars on their home cloud, which 10 players do we want on our team?

Q. What have you been smoking?

A. A regular team is what we're after. Not necessarily the 10 best players, but 10 who'd make a strong, aggressive team that played its best under pressure. We'd need four guards, four forwards and two centers. And a coach.

Q. Dare I ask? Have you chosen such a team?

A. I had trouble deciding who'd be eligible. I settled on players from Kentucky colleges — primarily because Kentuckians know them best, whether the players were born here or not. So a great one like Jeff Mullins, from Lexington, wasn't considered. He went to Duke University. As it happens, though, seven of my 10 players are Kentucky natives.

Q. Who's on the starting five?

A. The guards are Ralph Beard of Kentucky and Dwight Smith of Western Kentucky. Westley Unseld of Louisville is the center. Cliff Hagan and Dan Issel, both of UK, are the forwards.

Q. And the other five?

A. The second-team guards are Jim Price of Louisville and Frank Ramsey of Kentucky. The center is Alex Groza of Kentucky, and the forwards are Joe Fulks of Murray State and Charlie Tyra of Louisville.

Q. You don't have 10 per cent of a brain. What about Wah-Wah Jones? And Vernon Hatton and Clem Haskins? Louie Dampier, Dan Swartz, Jack Adams, Cotton Nash? You heard what Adolph said about Cotton's hands. How can you name 10 guys without Junior Bridgeman? Bill Spivey, for crying out loud. And Jim McDaniels, Duck Ray, LeRoy Edwards. What about —

A. Imagine my 10 guys in their prime. Put them all in a time machine and bring them out 25 years old. Beard is running

loose, a little man on fire. Smith is 6 feet 5, a defensive master, the perfect big-guard complement to Beard. We'll give Beard the ball, and Dwight will make St. Peter wish he'd drafted better.

Q. What about Kelly Coleman and Bob Burrow and Carlyle Towery and Pat Riley and Johnny Cox and John Turner? And —

A. Hagan and Issel will score from everywhere. Cliff is the better man inside because he's so quick and jumps so well. He'll score with tip-ins and little hook shots. Dan is a rarity, a big, strong man who can shoot from a distance. Again, the perfect complement to his running mate. And both Hagan and Issel can rebound, especially on the offensive board.

Q. — and Kevin Grevey? Wake up, man. You don't have Allen Murphy or Granny Williams or Jim Baechtold. Where's Don Goldstein, Butch Beard, Chuck Mrazovich?

A. Unseld isn't the tallest center available, and he isn't the scorer others are, but for a team like ours that is full of shooters we need that steady, unselfish, gifted athlete who will only get every rebound there is. That's Wes.

Q. Harold Sergeant, Odie Spears, Dee Gibson and Bud Olsen. Johnny Oldham and Bob Lavoy, Phil Rollins and Lou Tsioropolous. Aggie Sale, Mike Casey, Bill Lickert, Tom Marshall. You don't have five per cent of a normal man's gray matter. Jack Parkinson, Bob Mulcahy, Bobby Watson, Art Spoelstra.

A. If we need points in a hurry, we get Fulks in the game. He might be the best shooter ever in Kentucky. Tyra will be our enforcer, a brute who can rebound, score and make bruises. Groza can rebound with Tyra and he's twice the scorer. Imagine a front line of Unseld,

Groza and Tyra. They could kill buildings. Price and Ramsey are super guards at both ends of the floor. OK, Mr. Interviewer, any questions?

Q. What about the good players who helped Kentucky Wesleyan win four national college-division championships — Dallas Thornton, George Tinsley, Sam Smith? Kentucky State won three national championships with Elmore Smith and Travis Grant. Didn't a pro scout tell you in 1975 that Gerald Cunningham at Kentucky State was better than Grevey?

A. Any other questions?

Q. (Sighing.) So who's your coach?

A. Rupp. Give kindly old Adolph two months to get these 10 studs ready and St. Peter doesn't have a prayer, you should pardon the expression.

Q. All right, I give up. Tell me more about the team.

A. The Dream Team. Here's more...

First Five

Ralph Beard, 5-10, 170, University of Kentucky 1946-49. Born in Hardinsburg, Ky....All-State at Louisville Male High in 1944 and again in 1945, when Male won its first state championship... Three times All-America, twice the college Player of the Year...All-NBA in 1951.

If not for the point-shaving scandal, the glory that was Bob Cousy's may well have come to Beard. As contemporaries in college and then in the NBA — Beard a second-year pro when Cousy was a rookie — Beard always was superior.

His strengths were speed and quickness, a marvelous touch with either hand on the driving layup, a good two-handed set shot from six miles away, a nice 15-foot jumper made better by the threat of a drive, nerve-wracking defense — and the idea he was never going to lose a game.

Dwight Smith, 6-5, 190, Western

Ralph Beard for two.

Kentucky, 1965-67. Born in Princeton, Ky....All-State at Princeton Dotson where he averaged 22.3 points a game for three seasons....Averaged 14.6 points and 10.9 rebounds at Western, where he helped the team reach the NCAA Tournament twice.

Always in the shadow of All-America forward Clem (The Gem) Haskins, Smith reinforced his obscurity by not talking much. "He was shy," said John Oldham, the Western coach. "But on the floor he was our leader. He was the one who won big games for us." Oldham called Smith

191

Dwight Smith makes room.

the greatest rebounding guard in the nation. The Western publicity man, Ed Given, once a college basketball player and later a sports writer, said Smith was the best defensive guard he ever saw. "He'd force a man to make a bounce pass to his left — and then he'd steal the ball the second it touched the floor," Given said. "I thought it was an accident the first time I saw him do it. But he did it time after time." With a brilliant future ahead in the pros, Smith drowned in an automobile accident barely two months after his last game at Western.

Westley Unseld, 6-7, 240, University of Louisville, 1966-68. Born in Louisville.... Twice All-State at Louisville Seneca, which won back-to-back state championships. Twice All-America at Louisville, which won two conference championships and was rated No. 2 in the nation to UCLA and young Lew Alcindor....The NBA's Most Valuable Player as a rookie.

The Baltimore Bullets finished last in the NBA's Eastern Division in 1968. They won the whole shebang the next year. The team had changed by the addition of only one man — Unseld. He was the MVP not because he scored a lot (13.8 points a game), but because he rebounded, passed the ball out for a fast break while other guys were getting their feet untangled and played defense so strongly that even a mountain complained. Wilt Chamberlain, 7-1 and 300 pounds, said "&%$#!" And Unseld said, "I'm not going to talk to Wilt. Might make him mad." Doing his impression of the Colossus of Rhodes, Unseld set immovable picks for his gunning playmates. Imagine it. Unseld setting picks for Beard, Hagan and Issel. Dyn-o-mite.

Cliff Hagan 6-4, 200, Kentucky, 1951-54....Born in Owensboro, Ky....All-State

Westley Unseld on defense.

Cliff Hagan going up.

in 1948 and '49. Owensboro High won the state championship the second year.... All-America as a sophomore and senior (in between, UK was on suspension by the NCAA and didn't play a schedule).... 14 years a pro player, the 16th leading scorer ever when he left the NBA.

Bill Spivey, a 7-footer, was the college Player of the Year in 1951 when Kentucky won a national championship. UK's center the next year was Hagan, eight inches smaller — and he played the position better than Spivey had. Hagan was a work of art in the pivot, all grace and all strength, an extraordinary jumper with timing so good he could tip the ball from one side and, should it refuse to go in, tip it again from the other side. He scored on every kind of shot, but witnesses remember best the hook shot put up so smoothly the ball seemed to float.

Dan Issel, 6-8½, 240, Kentucky, 1968-70 . . . Born in Batavia, Ill. . . . Twice All-America . . . All-ABA as a rookie . . . Averaged over 20 points a game his first five years in the pros.

Issel broke Hagan's single-game scoring record of 51 with 53 against Mississippi in 1970. When Issel left UK to become a millionaire professional basketball player, he owned 35 other school records. He was Kentucky's all-time leading scorer, a big man who could score inside or on 18-foot jumpers. Harry Lancaster, for 20 years Rupp's right-hand man, said Issel was UK's best player ever. No one ever mistook Issel for a defensive genius, but who cares? For our team, Issel will put the ball in the hole.

Second Five

Jim Price, 6-3, 185, Louisville 1970-72....Born in Indianapolis....All-State at Indianapolis Tech....All-America in '72 when he led Louisville to the Final Four

Jim Price changes direction.

in the NCAA Tournament.

Two confrontations tell about Price, a master of defense who could score. Bo Lamar of Southwest Louisiana came into the '72 NCAA Midwest Regional with a large reputation as a gunner supreme. Against Price, Lamar needed 42 shots to make 14 while Price was 10-for-15. Bo threw up six — count 'em — air balls. Against UCLA's Henry Bibby, whose All-America credentials were impeccable and later certified by good work in the pros, Price beat him 30-2. Next case.

Frank Ramsey, 6-3, 185, Kentucky, 1951-54....Born in Madisonville, Ky....All-State in high school, All-America as a sophomore and senior....For nine years an integral part of a Boston Celtics dynasty that won seven NBA championships.

Irrepressible when moving the ball downcourt, Ramsey never wasted a moment on offense. Red Auerbach called him the best sixth man in history because Ramsey made things happen when he entered a game. More versatile than Hagan, Ramsey could play either out front or inside. He invented ways to get the ball in the bucket. Under pressure, he was majestic. If it's close at the end of our game with those heavenly all-stars, we need Beard and Ramsey in there together. Get this statistic: In the seven seasons Beard and Ramsey played at UK, the team won 214 games and lost 14.

Alex Groza, 6-7, 235, Kentucky, 1945-49....Born in Martins Ferry, Ohio.... All-America his last three years....Most Valuable Player in the 1948 and '49 NCAA tournaments won by UK....All-NBA both years with the Indianapolis Olympians.

He was 6-5 and 165 when Rupp gave him a scholarship. "Nobody else offered me one," Groza said. A year and a half in the Army made Groza a 6-7, 235-

Dan Issel is decisive.

pound strongman who, on return to UK, accomplished with force the little he couldn't do with his astonishing quickness. As a pro center, he was second only to George Mikan, who was later voted the Outstanding Player of the Half-Century. With Groza on our bench, coach Rupp has room to maneuver. Both Unseld and Groza, thanks to their wonderful agility, can play forward in a pinch.

Charlie Tyra, 6-8, 230, Louisville, 1955-57....Born in Louisville....All-State at Atherton High, where he set a city scoring record of almost 23 points a game....All-America in 1956 and MVP in the NIT won by Louisville....For seven years a pro with the New York Knickerbockers and Chicago Packers/Zephyrs.

They called him "Moose." In that big junior year, Tyra set both a school scoring record (23.8 points a game) and rebounding record (22.2 a game) that were on the books 20 years later. His offensive moves were limited because he wasn't as quick as Groza, say, but Tyra was valuable in the pros because of his unyielding defense and eager rebounding.

Joe Fulks, 6-4, 180, Murray State,

Frank Ramsey is behind LSU's Joe Dean (34).

1941-42....Born in Kuttawa, Ky....Took Kuttawa High to its only State Tournament appearance....Leading scorer in the first Kentucky-Indiana all-star high school basketball game....Led the NBA in scoring with a 23-point average in 1947 and set a single-game record of 63 points that lasted from 1949 to 1960.

His defense was mostly a shouted "Hey!," but he scored in bunches. His shots were distinguished by their fluffiness, as if he were throwing a cotton ball at the rim. They bounced there, and bounced and bounced, until, usually, they fell in. If St. Peter tries to zone our Dream Team, Fulks will fill up the basket in a rush.

Q. One more thing. What makes you think they play basketball in heaven?

A. If they play in Hell for Certain, I figure they must play in heaven for sure. As far as I can see, a heavenly basketball game would have only one problem.

Q. What's that?

A. Where would they get any referees?

Alex Groza scores in the 1948 NCAA championship game.

196

Joe Fulks

Charlie Tyra wears the MVP trophy in the 1956 NIT.

We wish to credit the following photographers:

C. Thomas Hardin pgs. 10, 16, 72-73, 76, 80, 94, 157 (top)
Ford Reid pgs. 11, 13 (top), 19, 20-21, 22, 24, 30, 44, 186
Carl Krull pg. 12
Barney Cowherd pgs. 12-13, 15, 58
Dave Kindred pg. 14
Billy Davis pg. 17
H. V. Withers pgs. 28, 104
Charley Pence pgs. 29, 52, 68, 69, 77, 99, 172 (top), 192, 193 (bottom)
Associated Press pgs. 32, 38, 92, 96, 109, 136, 191, 196, 197
Jim Wilson pg. 49 (bottom)
Gean Baron pgs. 49 (top), 54, 93
Charles Darneal pgs. 54-55
Al Hixenbaugh pg. 60 (right)
Al Blunk pgs. 60 (left), 63, 67, 116, 118, 195
Thomas V. Miller pgs. 61, 122-123, 129
Bud Kamenish pgs. 62, 65, 128, 156, 156-157, 163, 194 (bottom)
George Bailey pgs. 62-63, 81, 82, 114, 182
Larry Spitzer pgs. 68-69, 132, 133, 134, 140, 146, 180

Paul Schuhmann pg. 70
Bill Luster pgs. 75, 126, 128 (top), 130, 147, 151, 166 (top), 167, 175, 181
Jeff Watkins pgs. 76, 95
Bryan Moss pgs. 78-79, 150, 194 (top)
Ken Weaver pgs. 79, 153
University of Kentucky Archives pgs. 84 (bottom), 86, 89, 98, 102, 103, 184 (top)
Hugh Miller pg. 101
Margaret Hazel pg. 105 (top)
Robert Steinau pgs. 105 (bottom), 127
Western Kentucky University pgs. 119, 184 (bottom)
Centre College pg. 120
James Keen pgs. 125, 178 (top)
Keith Williams pgs. 145, 154, 155
Michael Coers pgs. 162, 166 (bottom)
Jim Harlan pgs. 165, 193 (top)
Frank Kimmel pg. 170
Melissa Farlow pg. 187
The Naismith Basketball Hall of Fame pg. 84
The University of Kansas pgs. 3, 84

INDEX